W0008542

Barry Trotter
and the
Unnecessary Sequel

Other Books By This *Idiot*

Barry Trotter and the Shameless Parody

How to Survive Being Shat Out Of a Bloody Great Dragon (*with Ruddy Hafwid*)

BARRY TROTTER
and the Unnecessary Sequel

Michael Gerber
(yes him again)

GOLLANCZ
LONDON

HEY YOU!

This is a work of parody. Any similarities, without satirical intent, to copyrighted characters/material, or individuals living or dead, is purely coincidental. This book has not been endorsed by J.K. Rowling, Bloomsbury Books, Warner Bros., or any of the other entities holding copyright or license to the Harry Potter books or films. No connection is implied or should be inferred. Of course, this notice itself could be parodic, in which case, it's anybody's guess as to what the hell is going on.

Seduced by some misguided vision of petty immortality, the moral right of Michael Gerber to be identified as the author of this shabby rot has been asserted by him in accordance with the Copyright, Designs and Patents Act of 1988. It would be funny, if it weren't so needy and sad.

First published in Great Britain in 2003 by Gollancz
A cynical, money-grubbing imprint of the Orion Publishing Group
Orion House, 5 Upper St Martin's Lane, London WC2H 9EA
(For a good time, ask for 'Ermine')

Typeset by Deltatype Ltd, Birkenhead, Merseyside

Grudgingly printed in Great Britain by Clays Ltd, St Ives, plc
'Don't blame us – we only printed it'

A CIP catalogue record for this book is available from the British Library

ISBN 0 575 07558 9

To Kate, who knows something funny when she reads it,

all the Trotteristas who demanded another one

. . . and, of course, to YOU![1]

[1] (but only if you paid for it)

A Note To Sensitive Readers

This book contains extremely graphic descriptions of sex, often without cuddling. Its needlessly frank, obsessively detailed sexual language – and diagrams – render this book COMPLETELY UNSUITABLE for sensitive readers.

In fact, only that small clutch of sweaty-palmed perverts bent on imagining beloved icons of their childhood 'getting it on' in every conceivable fashion, for the flimsiest of reasons, should purchase this book. You know who you are.

– *The Publisher*

This book has been copyedited by the blind. Since 1961, the Oedipus Foundation has been helping Britain's sight-impaired find work in all fields of manuscript preparation. When you buy a book copyedited by the blind, you're sending a message: 'I caree.'

CONTENTS

Chapter One

A BIRTHDAY, AND A BOOK

Barry Trotter had always had awful birthdays. By thirty-eight, it had become a perverse point of pride with him, like the grottiness of his attire had been during his teens, or merciless sarcasm in his twenties. 'You want a *present*, boy?' his Uncle Vermon used to drawl malevolently. 'How about not killing you? How's *that* for a present?' Sure, Barry had the last laugh – but you can't humiliate, drive insane, and ultimately crucify memories.

These days things were only slightly better. He could count on getting another squeaky fire hydrant from Lonald Measly, his dog-brained pal. A biohazard-suited postman would bring a few exuberantly lethal candies from Ferd, and a bloody-minded trick something-or-other from Jorge. His godfather Serious Blech would send him a birthday card, not containing money, but asking for some. And he'd get something incredibly useful and completely boring from his wife Ermine Cringer. What would it be this year? Recent hints suggested a self-scrubbing wok. Even a Strip-O-Gram was too much to hope for, now that they had kids.

'Thirty-eight down, hundreds more of these miserable buggers to go,' Barry said, shutting off his computer at the Ministry of Magicity, where he was assistant deputy under-vice-secretary for Muddle relations. Earlier in the day – wasting time as usual – he typed 'thirty-eight' into the wizard search engine, *prest.org*: 'According to Nostradamus, this number symbolises the little-known Fifth Horse of the Apocalypse, Boredom.'

As far as Barry could tell, his family had totally forgotten. Ermine was (to use her phrase) 'busy living her *life*'. At the moment, that meant writing a syndicated advice column, 'Ermine's 'Elps', for the *Daily Soothsayer*. In it, she perkily suggested witchy uses for Muddle stuff. 'If a potion calls for a horse's hoof, use store-bought gelatin instead!' On Tuesdays and Thursdays, Ermine wafted the five minutes into Oxford to teach a gorilla named Audrey how to cast spells; this was part of a PhD in Cryptozoology.[1] And in spare moments –

[1] In the wizarding world, teaching a gorilla magic was about as illegal as you could get without splitting Time into seventeen

most weekends, the evenings, in the bath – she was translating *The Book of Common Spells* into 133+-speak. Add to this the constant supervision and improvement of their children, Nigel (eleven) and Fiona (three), and any normal person would give Ermine a pass.

But Barry wasn't normal, and Ermine knew it. Each of his birthdays was a minefield of unspoken expectations – and Barry wasn't above withholding sex if he wasn't well pleased. Every 31 July, she spiked Barry's morning cuppa with Maturi-tea, just to take the edge off; Ermine shuddered to think what Barry would've been like 'straight'. Magicking your spouse was frowned on – some little niggle involving free will – but being married to Barry Trotter called for desperate measures. Besides, the tantrum of a powerful wizard could ding up an ecosystem. Every married couple plays by their own set of rules, and Ermine's included the occasional misdemeanour in the name of sanity and the greater good.

different dimensions and committing crimes in all of them simultaneously. Barry took some credit for turning the former Miss Perfect Cringer into such a rebel; but of course her curiosity had always been her strongest attribute. Barry had to admit that the gorilla was learning staggeringly fast. After just six months, Audrey had several of the deadliest spells known to wizardry down cold. As a result, nobody messed with her cat, 'All-Ball'. (They did, however, say what a stupid name that was – behind her back.)

Ermine remembered that it was her husband's birthday a little after four, only an hour and a half before he arrived home. The kids were immediately set to making cards (she'd cast a quick Clumsy Sweetness spell on them if necessary), while Ermine sent owls to all their pals.

While she waited for responses, Ermine polished off today's column. She needed ten more words. 'Old, unenchanted pantyhose can be really, really, really, really, useful,' she typed, and tapped the screen with her wand – the column was sent to her editor, a crusty old warlock named Clagton who smelled like newsprint and bats' blood pomade.

Ermine spent the next hour conjuring like mad – a few presents, a cake, some hats and decorations. Since everything has to come from somewhere, these things disappeared from various Muddle stores, the Sharper Mage, a Muddle bakery,[2] and the party of an unlucky seven-year-old in China.

The responses trickled in, with the mean old Measly owl Ahole grudgingly delivering a birthday card as

[2] Which was about to be closed for health-code violations. The spell didn't care – it got what you asked for, regardless of quality. Therefore, it was important to be specific. 'A *nice* coat.' 'A birthday cake *without* rat droppings.'

well. He'd straggled in, probably drunk, daring Ermine not to give him a treat, and lunging for her jugular when she did. She and Ahole were old adversaries, and she'd had a tennis racket on hand. 'Tell Ferd to send Herpes next time,' Ermine said, knocking Ahole outside with an overhead smash.[3]

Promptly at five, several hastily assembled guests had collected at the Trotters' small home. Lon was there, minded as usual by his sister Genny. Ahole had conveyed Ferd and Jorge's regrets – the twins were in the middle of blowing up a small, petulant country on behalf of NATO. But Lord Valumart made it.

'Thanks, Terry,' Ermine said when she greeted the Dork Lord at the door. 'Barry will appreciate it. We know how rarely you travel.'

'I was in the neighbourhood, shutting down some unprofitable orphanages,' Valumart said. 'It's important to stop and smell the roses once in a while, you know?'

Ermine smiled weakly. Valumart had grown ever richer, and weirder with every pound, dollar, drachma or zloty that poured in. He lived in the penthouse suite of Nero's Gardens, a posh hotel/casino in Hogsbleede,

[3] The Measlys didn't have very good luck with owls. Lon had once owned a tiny anal-retentive one named Prig (short for Prigrigid), which he ate soon after his dog-brain transplant.

Sin City of the wizarding world. Valumart was Hogsbleede's unofficial mayor and de facto monarch.[4]

At one time always spiffily dressed in a black tunic jammed with phony medals, Valumart now shuffled around with tissueboxes on his feet. If he wanted to grow his fingernails two feet long and wear a surgical mask, who was going to stop him? Valumart owned most of the town, and before being dismissed as Chancellor of the Exchequer, he was able to have Hogsbleede declared autonomous, so that he couldn't be extradited. But all that Muddle money was buying him a curse, the curse of never hearing 'no'. He didn't even care enough to put on a fruity fake German accent any more.

[4] Hogsbleede was a gilded bog, a nasty bit of nowhere puffed up by the power of vice. Wizards loved to gamble, and so the casinos made a killing – as long as they kept an eye out for seers. (For example, Mrs Tralala, Hogwash's Diviation Teacher, was *Medea non grata* at the gaming tables.) As for the pleasures of the flesh, the tricks a magical prostitute knew were enough to make the average client swallow his or her tongue. Magical prostitutes, all licensed incubi and succubi, were strictly regulated by a Ministry department (headed by Tarty Crotch). They had a tremendously powerful union, being willing to exercise the Lysistrata option when necessary. In fact, in 1612 a strike by all the Goblin blackjack dealers almost strangled Hogsbleede in its dirty little cradle, after the sex workers went out in sympathy. That hit the wizards where it hurt, and they had to settle.

This might surprise you, He-Who-Smells showing up at a birthday party for Barry Trotter. But you'd be amazed at how much constantly trying to kill someone can feel like – yes, I'll say it! – a love affair. Barry considered him a charming rogue, a snake-oil salesman who happened to sell phony phoenix tears instead. (The stick-in-your-brain jingles oozed powerful Dork magic: 'You hurt yourself/Whatta shame/Try Cryin' Flame/Ask for it . . . by name!')

Valumart always brought a little something for the kids; this time it was a slot machine magically connected to the United States Mint. 'Get them young, and you have a customer for life,' he always said.

They all waited in the front room, listening for Barry's footfall outside the door. He wore seven-league wingtips, so they wouldn't get much warning.

Ermine turned to Valumart to make small talk, trying to put his odd personal smell out of her mind. 'How was the trip down?'

'Fine, fine.' Valumart was taking a risk by leaving Hogsbleede – in addition to the inevitable back taxes and Ponzi spells, the Muddles wanted to throw him in the clink for an internet scam involving some mythical funds trapped in Nigeria. Mind you, if the frankincense ever really hit the fan, he could always evaporate and literally slip through their fingers.

Valumart laughed and pointed. Red-haired Fiona, very magical for her age, was levitating her rune blocks and flinging them at her older brother, Nigel, who had been trying to rig the slot machine.

'Ow!' Nigel hollered, getting one in the eye. Then another just above the ear. 'Fi, stop it!'

Picking up on the conflict, Lon's frenzied barks came from the bathroom. He was celebrating the cocktail hour by drinking from the toilet.

'Shh, Lon! Quiet down!' Genny[5] Measly told her big brother. Still unmarried (Barry always suspected her brush with the basilisp had something to do with it), she took care of Lon, feeding him, making sure he got his walkies.

Laughing, Fiona sent over more blocks, and faster. Nigel took his appeal directly to the High Court. 'Mum! Tell her to stop!'

'Stop fighting, you two.' With a finger, Ermine brought a levitating tray of potions in for a landing on the coffee table. In a corner, several presents had got into the drinks cabinet and were unwrapping each other and giggling.

'We *aren't* fighting, she's hitting me with blocks. The

[5] Short for 'Genital,' her mother's rather unfortunate maiden name.

difference is subtle but, I believe, meaningful,' Nigel complained. As verbal as his sister was magical, Nigel would start at Hogwash School of Wizardry and Witchcrap in a month. He was the spitting image of his father, except for that famous interrobang. Nigel had no early warning system, so Life constantly sucker-punched him.

Valumart was determined to fix Nigel up. 'Nigel, come here,' he said, reaching into his pocket and rummaging around. 'I want to give you a' – Valumart looked in his palm to see what he had to offer – 'a piece of lint. It is . . .' Valumart paused, searching for a selling point, '. . . very magical and charming.'

'No, thanks, "Uncle" Terry,' Nigel said, keeping his distance. 'I've got enough magical stuff already.' He saw Valumart's decidedly old-school pocketknife, a holdover from his Teutonic dress-up days – it looked wickedly sharp, and had a small skull on the end of it. Sometimes you didn't need an interrobang to know which way the wind was blowing.

But the Dork Lord was undeterred, and kept rummaging. 'No, really, I've got something very enjoyable for you. An old movie ticket? A scrap of paper that says' – Valumart unfolded it – '"Dominate world" on it?'

Too polite to tell an adult to piss off, Nigel tried to

change the subject. 'Hey Mum, can I get red contact lenses?'

Suddenly, Lon ran in from the bathroom and howled. 'Lonald, shhh!' Genny said. Lon ran to the door. He had a little hand-lettered 'Happy Birthday Barry' pennant stuck in his head-hole. There were steps on the stair, then a wand tap on the lock, and Barry walked in.

'Surprise!' everybody yelled, and Barry was. He smiled.

As befitting an adult, Barry's haul was modest, but heartfelt. From Lon and Genny he got a subscription to *Lay Off!*, England's leading professional Quiddit weekly. Valumart got him a magical hair-thickening comb.

'See, it works!' Valumart said, shaking his long, unwashed locks. Barry's hair was just as untidy as ever, but now there was less of it – or his head was growing, which didn't make sense. (For one thing, his home-made beer helmet still fit perfectly.)

Fiona got him – via Ermine, of course – a pair of yellow flannel pyjamas covered with purple moons and stars. (Gay with a side order of retarded,[6] Barry

[6] Or, to be more politically correct, 'These clothes practise an alternative lifestyle, and have special needs!'

thought, but smiled just the same.) From Nigel, Barry got a Sneaky Prickoscope, a device for telling whether people were jerks. 'Useful,' he said, and his son beamed (he had picked it out himself – or, more accurately, told his mum what to conjure from the Sharper Mage catalogue).

'You'd better not take that to work,' Ermine said. 'It'll go off all day long. Do you like the babble-band?'

Barry knew enough to say the right thing. 'I do, it's great . . . What is it?'

'I thought it might be useful on the phone,' his wife said. 'It's a little ribbon worn around the tongue like dith—' She spread it across her fingers and stuck them in her mouth.

'Gross, Erm,' Genny said.

'I wasn't going to *do* it,' she said (but she was – Ermine was the kind of person who ate from other people's plates). 'It allows you to speak whatever language somebody is speaking to you. Anyway, your real present is tonight,' she whispered, and kissed his cheek.

Nigel heard. 'Gross!' he said, disgusted to his core.

'Goss!' his sister mimicked.

'But how can you understand *them*?' Genny said.

'I never thought of that,' Ermine said, slightly annoyed. 'Maybe they make earmuffs?' She suspected that Genny resented her having stolen Barry. Yes, Barry had once been a prize, though you wouldn't have known it to look at him now. He was scratching himself.

'Barry, not in front of the guests,' Ermine pleaded.

'It's my birthday, I can do what I please,' he said. Barry held up a birthday hat. 'Why do the party hats have pictures of Mao on them?'

After the cake (which read 'Congratulations on Your Retirement') Ermine said, 'It's such a nice evening. Why don't we move the party into the garden?' They'd been lucky so far, but it was only a matter of time before Lon got overexcited and widdled on the rug.

Barry excused himself for a moment and went to the kitchen – being around Valumart always gave him a scar-ache. The only thing that worked was Ermine's menstrual aspirin, which also kept him from bloating.

He was just washing down a few tablets at the kitchen sink when something caught his eye through the window.

'Ermine, that bloody urchin is back again!'

'Oh, leave her alone, Barry,' Ermine said. 'I've seen her around the College. Everybody calls her Liar.' You had to have a thick skin to work at the school, which was crawling with vomiting undergrads, dippy American tourists, and plucky preteens having inscrutable adventures in multidimensional Miltonian cosmologies.

Barry was implacable. 'Hey, you! Dirtbag! Get out of here!' She was a little blonde girl, dressed adequately, but strangely undomesticated. 'And take your ferret—'

'It's not a ferret, ya tosser!' she shouted. 'It's an expression of my inner self in animal form!'

'Well, your inner self poos in our garden!' Barry retorted. The girl stuck her tongue out at him, then clambered over the back wall.

'This neighbourhood!' Barry said. 'First the witch two streets down . . .' (The witch in question had been cooked and eaten by children; luckily, her life insurance covered 'Malicious Consumption by Minors'.)

'They found the kids who did it,' Ermine said. 'Germans,' she added meaningfully, as if that explained everything.

The group brought chairs out on to the grass. Barry passed the Measlys' ancient Ford Ganglia, now passed down to Genny.[7] Reaching in through an open

[7] After the boys had crashed it, the enchanted vehicle spent ten years tooling around ferally in the Forsaken Forest. At some point, it had met an abandoned Mini and, with her, sired a bunch of

window – an enticement to thieves that had so far proved unsuccessful – Barry jabbed the Implausibility Booster. It was still broken.

'Lon, do you remember when we flew this hunk of junk into the Buggering Birch?' Barry said, suddenly misty. He was a nostalgia addict. 'I couldn't sit down for a week.'

'Yeah,' said Lon absently. He was on his hands and knees, sniffing a tree trunk.

'I've heard good things about those Dragonette Decimators,' Ermine said, out of the blue. Barry didn't respond. She was constantly on about this latest fad in wizard cars. 'I need one for safety,' she always said, but Barry suspected it was because Penelope Saggs had one. Penelope made a lot of money selling property in other dimensions.

'Lon, don't wee on the lawn,' Genny told her brother. 'It'll kill the grass.'

'It'll make the Muddles next door call the cops,' Barry said. Once secretive, magical folk lived openly among Muddles now, mostly harmoniously. But there were limits, and Lon whipping it out definitely crossed one.

mopeds. The Ganglia needed to pay child-support, so it went back to the Measlys.

They all arranged their chairs. 'Go and sit next to Uncle Terry,' Ermine told Nigel.

'He's going to carve my head,' Nigel whispered.

'Oh, shush,' Ermine said. 'Uncle Terry likes you.'

'Undoubtedly! Look – he's brought a portable woodburning kit!' It was true – a wisp of smoke curled skyward as he carved 'H-W-S is No. 1' in the arm of the lawn chair.

Ermine waved her hand dismissively. 'Oh, he's probably trying to be funny. You know what a weird sense of humour he has.'

'But Mum—'

'No buts. His feelings will be hurt,' Ermine said.

Nigel plopped down, and took a glum drink from his disgusting tannis-root squash (it was supposed to make him more magical). Lon circled three times and laid down next to the boy. Fiona was investigating an old lollipop left in the grass, prior to eating it.

'Icky!' Ermine said. 'Put that down.'

'I wa' icky!' Fiona said, outraged. She made the hem of her mother's skirt smoulder.

'Who wants an early bed time?' Ermine threatened. The smouldering stopped.

Barry had gone back into the house and brought out a little dry-erase board. He wrote something on it, then put it next to him and tilted the board towards the sky.

Valumart read the message: 'Will Be Probed For Food.'

'Dad wants to get abducted by aliens,' Nigel said to Valumart.

'Pardon me,' the Dork Lord said, 'since the sign is between us – just so there is no confusion –' He drew an arrow pointing in the proper direction. 'I hate those little bastards,' Valumart said. 'I can't *sell* them anything.'

'When did you decide to get abducted, Barry?' Genny asked.

'Oh, after they fired me at Hogwash.' His book, *Barry Trotter and the Shameless Parody,* written while he was Public Relations Officer for Hogwash, had indeed got the school lots of publicity. Unfortunately, all of it was bad.

'Do you remember what Nigel asked when you told us about your plan for being abducted?' Ermine said. '"Is there any money in that?"'

Everybody laughed at the boy's precocity except Nigel himself. He had honestly wondered.

Ermine continued. 'I was overjoyed at the possibility of getting him out of the house,' she said. 'Two weeks and it looked like the whole place had suffered an epileptic fit.'

'Yeah, she offered to pack me a lunch. Too bad I

didn't need it,' Barry said glumly. 'They wouldn't take me.' The hopeful space traveller had sat out on the front lawn for a week, an overnight bag next to him, with a supply of chocolates and beer for sustenance.

'They won't take magical folk,' Ermine said. 'Not good enough for them, I suppose.'

'They're bloody prejudiced!' Barry said, taking an angry swig of his Boarsbollocks' Brew, and pumping a fist into the air. 'We Shall Overcome!'

'Have you tried reverse psychology?' Genny asked, trying to be helpful.

This made sense, so Barry wiped the board and wrote, 'Please DON'T Abduct Me.'

'Cunning.' Valumart said. You often couldn't tell whether he was making fun of you or not, Barry thought. Maybe that's why he didn't have many friends. 'If they don't take me this time, I'm going to get really drunk, find a flying saucer and puke on it.'

'Understandable,' Valumart said.

'Anyway, I'm glad Barry has a job now,' Ermine said. 'Getting abducted's a hobby, not a career.'

'Thank goodness for the Ministry,' Genny said. 'No offence,' she said to Lord Valumart.

'None taken,' Valumart said. 'The Ministry of Magicity is a necessary good.'

'Well, you didn't have to be at work with me today,' Barry said bitterly.

'Why? What did you have to do?' Valumart asked. Dusk was falling.

'Bloody boring public service announcement,' he said. When Barry Trotter spoke, Muddles listened. Today what he was saying was, 'Don't cast bootleg spells.' For the past several years, Dork wizards had been providing blackmarket spells, or 'charmz', catering to Muddles' every desire, from finding a mate to automotive repair. The problem was that these spells had been copied so many times, from smudgy parchments full of archaic words, they were full of errors. So a love charm aimed at the girl next door might light on your older brother instead. Or an incantation to increase your height would actually make the entire outside world slightly *smaller*.

'What were you saying today?' Genny said, with a touch of hero-worship. 'Can you still remember it?'

'God, I'll never forget it,' Barry said. 'Three hundred takes. "Read 'em, trade 'em, collect 'em – just don't say 'em. Magic isn't a toy and charmz can be deadly,"' Barry parroted with a glazed look in his eye. 'Behind me, there was this wall of televisions playing an endless loop of some poor kid getting his eyeballs pulled out by an imp.'

'Ooh, how awful.' Genny stood up and stretched. 'Well, people, we'd best be going. Lon gets me up at the crack of dawn.'

'Thanks for coming, Genny,' Barry said. 'And thanks for letting us take Lon to school for the Reunion next month.'

'Quite all right,' Genny said. 'I think he'll enjoy it and, frankly, I could use the time off. Taking care of a half-canine manchild can be wearing.'

'I understand more than you realise,' Ermine said. Barry elbowed her.

After Genny and Lon had left, Barry asked Valumart, 'Are you coming to the Reunion?'

The Dork Lord laughed. 'Of course not! I wasn't a member of your class.'

'Yes, but you spent so much time trying to kill us . . . if anybody deserves to be an honorary member, it's you,' Ermine said.

'I graduated four years later, and they're letting me go,' said Barry.

'But I'm not the great Barry Trotter,' Valumart said.

'Nor am I,' Barry said, smirking. 'Those books were mostly nonsense. You know that.'

'You always stayed one step ahead of *me*,' he replied. For an evil mastermind, Lord Valumart was certainly a good sport. 'Speaking of books,' Valumart said, 'I have a proposition for you. I'd like you to do another one.'

'Why?' Barry asked. 'My latest royalty statement said we hadn't broken twenty copies yet.' (It had actually spoken – magical world, and all that.)

'And we never will,' Valumart said. 'That's precisely why I'm asking. ValuBooks needs to lose some serious money before year's end or the taxman will have my arse. That damn "*Wizard Called It*" book is flying out of the stores.'

'It's true,' Ermine chimed in. 'The last time I was at Boorish and Clots, one hit me.' She showed a bruise.

'A kid in my class was browsing in Wartytoad's and got a broken nose,' Nigel said.

Valumart chuckled. Other people's injuries amused him. 'Anyway, I need to lose some money, so naturally I thought of you.'

'Thanks, I think,' Barry said. 'What did you have in mind, another parody?'

'God no,' Valumart said. 'I don't need to lose that much. A small outrage will do – maybe a memoir or something?'

Valumart tapped a pack of cigarettes on the arm of the chair, and took one out. He offered it to Nigel, who declined.

'Why do you smoke?' Ermine said. 'It's so bad for you.'

'The alternative is living with Muddles for four hundred years, and I need to cling to something,' the Dork Lord said. He pulled down his surgical mask and lit up. 'What about some sort of tell-all, where you set the record straight, in your own words?'

'How straight?' Ermine asked, worry creeping in.

'Don't worry, Ermine, not that straight,' Valumart said, smiling. His spies had once given him a single-spaced list of Ermine's schoolgirl crushes, flirts, dalliances and affairs. It weighed twelve pounds.

'Oh, I don't think anybody'd be interested—' Barry began.

'Precisely,' Valumart said, shaking his match out and throwing it into the grass. It was magical, so it kept burning. Only Nigel saw it, and for the rest of the evening he battled the flame alone, with spit.

'Okay,' Barry said. 'I'll try to come up with something.'

'Great,' Valumart said. 'You do that. I'm sure it will be a worst-seller.'

Something caught Ermine's eye. 'Hey! Look out!'

A lump of metal fell from the sky and hit Barry squarely on the forehead.

'Ow!' Barry said, clutching his noggin. Nigel had grabbed Fiona and scrambled under his chair.

'Barry, are you okay?' Ermine asked.

'It's those damn aliens,' Valumart said. 'They've really got it in for you.'

Rubbing his injury – which was already beginning to swell – he turned the piece of metal over. 'Give me that match, Nigel,' he said. Looking at it in the flickering light, Barry read what had been incised – in perfect cursive – on the piece of slag: 'Wishing you were here . . .'

With a swoosh, another lump of metal hit him, this time on the backside, as eerily accurate as the first. 'Ow! *Alpo!*' Barry swore. (For the sake of the children, he and Ermine had agreed to replace all instances of 'the f word' with their ex-Headmister's name.) Immediately Barry whipped his wand out, pointed upwards in the direction of the attack, and yelled.

'*Aveda Neutrogena!*' The infamous death-by-moisturising spell spurted out into the inky black. They were well out of range; it would fall in viscous green clumps all over the garden for the rest of the night.

Somewhat avenged, he looked at the new missile, which bore a single word.

'*Psyche*!'

Chapter Two

SPECIAL BRANCH

Barry still had quite a knot on his forehead the next day. He tried to cover it with his hair, but there simply wasn't enough.

'You look like a beluga whale,' Ermine said.

'Not helping,' Barry said in an annoyed sing-song, as he and Nigel walked out of the front door. They were going on a special VIP tour of 'Special Branch', the secret Muddle department which tried to minimise the effects wizarding folk had on the non-magical world. It was what Barry did, except from the other end. Not long after he began his job, Barry got a courtesy call from a Mr Nicholas Henratty, inviting him to come in and see how 'we Muddles tackle the magic problem'. It had taken Barry a while to find his feet at work – paper-shuffling wasn't Quiddit – but a few months later he called Henratty back to take him up on the offer.

'May I bring my son?' Barry had said. 'I know it's top-secret and all, but he loves Muddles.'

'What's his name?' Henratty asked. He sounded efficient, the kind of can-do executive who could type his own letters if necessary. Barry was still mastering the finer points of the 'Caps Lock' key.

'Nigel,' Barry said.

'Only if Nigel promises to blab about everything he sees to his wizard pals,' Henratty replied. 'The more wizards know about how much trouble their magic causes, the easier it will be for everybody. It's especially important to get to young wizards, before they start casting. We have to teach them that every spell has an impact.'

'Oh, right, absolutely.' Barry felt a pang of guilt over the incredible mayhem he must have caused in his life, and a desire to put it right – then felt an equally strong desire for whatever was cooking in the office pantry. (Sometimes a super-short attention span was a blessing.) 'Wednesday morning, then. We'll be looking forward to it.'

A witch's brew of hard work, persistent lying, and Muddle inattentiveness had kept the wizarding world secret for centuries. But that was before a Muddle journalist named J.G. Rollins took a spot-ravaged, hormone-addled young wizard with poor impulse control and transformed him into the idol of millions. Overnight, Barry Trotter became an international celebrity and threat to hotel rooms everywhere. Equally overnight, every aspect of the wizarding world was exposed.

Whenever the phenomenon looked as though it was about to die down, and people like Dirdy Dimsley or Dorco Malfeasance could eat in restaurants without fending off butterknife-wielding preteens, another book would come out and another wave of Trottermania would envelop the world. The inevitable flotilla of movies upped Barry's profile so insanely that during one memorable month he was given an Oscar, a Grammy, and elected to play power forward in the NBA's All-Star Game (whatever that was).

The success was relentless, and it changed things for ever. J.G. herself went from just another magic groupie being chucked out of the Dork Wizards convention at Davos, Switzerland, to somebody whose bank account required several pounds' worth of extra zeros. Barry himself got more famous than rich; but J.G.'s generosity made sure he and his wife would never want for cauldron cleanser.

If this state of affairs was indirectly Barry's fault, his pal Lord Valumart had a lot to answer for, too. He-

Who-Smells had spent all of Barry's preposterously extended school days trying to do away with the lad – so incessantly, in fact, that Headmister Bumblemore eventually refused to accept assassination attempts as an excuse for late work. Valumart wanted to murder Barry solely out of anal-retentiveness, having killed Barry's parents in December 1980. Sure, Valumart felt bad after his personal Concorde crashed into the Trotters' enchanted VW microbus high over Rendlesham Forest. But it wasn't his fault; the van's psychedelic paint job made it nearly invisible to radar – the inquiry said so. Still, with Priapus and Lunenestra Trotter[8] out of the way, Valumart figured that a clean slate was better for all concerned, and his lawyers agreed: no pesky next of kin, no lawsuits.

But Barry proved wily and tough, with a special knack for the ancient 'I'm Rubber and You're Glue'

[8] Ironically, Lily and James Trotter adopted these ridiculous names – to them, the height of cool – to show their disapproving families that they were mature, responsible adults ready for the commitment of marriage. Unfortunately, all it got them was surveillance from the drug squad of the local police. (In 1977, Barry's father was arrested for possessing a dealable quantity of myrrh.) They remained steadfast, doe-eyed members of the patchouli and no-deodorant set until the day they died. They met at a Seals and Crofts concert in 1974; Priapus was trying to hawk 'genuine Beatle reunion 8-tracks'.

spell. Valumart eventually saw that there were benefits to keeping the boy around. After the mammoth success of the movie *Barry Trotter and the Inevitable Attempt to Cash In,* Lord Valumart and his Earth Eater cronies switched tactics, realising that there was serious money to be made selling wizard stuff to Muddles. And so a cross-cultural fleecing began.

With his earlier fiendishness – muzak, credit cards, even the shock-rock of Valid Tumour Alarm – Valumart had kept his involvement secret. Now, he milked magicalness for all it was worth. In the words of the *Financial Times,* he became the 'world's Placebo King', happy to provide some squirt of completely inactive ingredients that Muddles couldn't even finish before asking for seconds. When twelve Muddles died from one of his Enchanted Habenero Enemas, Valumart was unapologetic: 'Wizard products only cause injury if you deserve it . . . They are by their nature incomprehensible to Muddle science. You can test them for safety no more than an airline mechanic can inspect a flying carpet.'

Regardless, magical folk were encouraged to 'come out' to their Muddle friends and neighbours, and most of them did. Witches and wizards got a lot more conventional-looking, and acting. Perhaps the goal was to bore the Muddles into submission, but the truth was a lot of the fun in dressing and acting weird disappears once everybody starts doing it. The idea was that magical folk were just like you and me, if you and I could cast spells, conjure things, levitate, talk to animals, see the future, teleport, and even shoot laserbeams out of our eyes (after a well-chosen bit of Latin or Yiddish, of course).

So the two worlds had become one. The old Ministry of Magicity was obsolete – after Trottermania, keeping Muddles ignorant of the wizarding world was like bailing the Atlantic with a paper cup. Its members quietly dispersed, and those few who stayed turned their efforts towards that particularly Muddle form of magic, public relations. Integration was the watchword, and while every wizard didn't agree with it, no one could present an alternative.

Among the handful of people employed to put forth this idea was your friend and mine, the world's most famous wizard, Barry Trotter. Now anybody who knew the real Barry, as opposed to J.G. Rollins's much more appealing creation, would be appalled. Even at thirty-eight, the lapses in Barry's judgement were so frequent that the brief periods of sensible behaviour were the exception, not the rule. Though his earlier impulses towards greed, gluttony, torpor and untidiness had been moderated by age, this was due more to a general lessening of energy than any positive change. Not that Barry was a bad fellow – he was always ready to a tell a fictitious story, dispense bad advice, or lend an inexpert hand. It's just that he was sort of a loose cannon. A very loose, very, very big cannon that fired nuclear-tipped artillery shells. Into heavily populated areas. At dinner time. In other words, precisely not the sort of fellow you'd want anywhere near the delicate essentials of Muddle/wizard relations.

For as much good will as there was between Muddles and wizards, the two groups were not equal, and never could be. There was an unspoken thicket of fear between them; Muddle leaders feared wizards' power, and the wizards lived in fear of the mob. People like Barry and Henratty did their very best to keep this delicate system in balance, because the alternative was – well, nobody wanted to think about that.

The morning of their trip to Special Branch, Nigel was more excited than Barry had ever seen him. He didn't even complain when Fiona, as usual, sprayed her porridge all over him. (His satchel was positively stiff with the stuff.)

Nigel even consented to taking the Magic Bus, a major concession. He didn't like to use magical ways of getting around. They made him too nervous.

'I don't understand,' Barry said as they rode into London. 'A Ford Ganglia is much more dangerous.'

'Yeah, the way you drive it,' Nigel said, nose in a comic book.

'You're going to have to get over your phobias sooner or later,' Barry said as they rode along.

'I know,' Nigel scraped at some dried porridge with a thumbnail.

'It's all in your head, son,' Barry said. Next to him, the ghost of Keith Moon was spitting champagne at passing cars.

'What about those studies that say using magic makes you sterile?' Nigel said.

'Do I look sterile?' Barry said.

'I don't know, I've never looked,' Nigel said.

'I don't trust that dodgy Muddle scientific method. Now, if a reputable wizard had told me, "Listen, don't stow your wand near your willie," then I'd think twice.'

'Crazy, then. You can't deny that magic makes you crazy,' Nigel said. 'Look at Alpo.[9]'

[9] After being replaced as Hogwash's Headmister, Alpo Bumblemore began a second career on Valumart's new magic-focused cable channel. However, the Iron Chef-like alchemy competition Alpo hosted lasted for only three unwatchable episodes. ('No Boffs For Toff Prof,' the *Stun* gloated.) He became an occasional talking head on the chat shows, but this, too, ended badly. On a show discussing

'One man doesn't prove anything,' Barry replied.

'You, Mum, Uncle Serious, the Measlys – all you wand-weasels are weirdoes.'

'"Wand-weasel" is such an ugly term. How would you like it if I called one of your Muddle pals a Mudbutt?'

'Well, they are crazy.'

Barry could not argue with his son's pre-adolescent moral clarity, so he changed the subject. 'Maybe so, but you'll have to do magic sooner or later.' Nigel didn't respond; he was engrossed in an ad for five thousand enchanted toy soldiers that screamed and shat themselves.

When they got to the London address Henratty had given them, all they saw was a small plot of well-tended grass with a large tree on it. Barry stepped over the low iron fence and approached the tree.

'Dad, the sign says "Keep Off the Grass",' Nigel said, eyeing an approaching policeman.

'That's just for dogs,' Barry said.

Nearly £1000 worth of official cautions later – DC

the topic 'Wizards – the New Amish?' a drunken Bumblemore had accused another guest, the wizard Gandolt, of being 'a sell-out' for going on tour with Led Zeppelin. Gandolt replied by accusing Bumblemore of 'stealing his look', and the two upended the table and grappled before a hooting studio audience. Bumblemore got the worst of it. Humiliated, he disappeared. Nobody had a clue where he'd gone to; the Ministry listed him as 'missing, presumed annoying.'

Kyriakou took over, after PC Cootes's hand got tired during the fourteenth citation –[10] Barry finally pulled the correct tree limb in the correct way, and a hidden door slid open. 'Come on,' he said, and he and Nigel descended some stairs into a reception area.

'We're here to see Mr Henratty,' Barry said.

'Please take a seat,' the receptionist said. 'I'll let him know you've arrived.'

Mr Henratty was a rumpled, harassed-looking, slightly portly man, somebody whose job was so demanding that the niceties of personal maintenance had to take a back seat to efficiency. He shaved his head, for example, to save time on haircuts; owned a week's worth of identical suits; he even tried to use as many contractions as possible when he talked. There were so many wizards doing so many spells, and there was so little time. However, as much as the job beat him down, an inner spark remained. There was a merriness about his face, especially his mouth, which turned up in the corners to give him a

[10] Here's how it happened: Barry got on the grass, and the cops gave him an official caution. He waited until he thought they weren't looking, then tried again. They caught him again. He had Nigel create a diversion. They caught him again. He tried to hide in the bushes. They caught him again. He tried to run across the grass as fast as he could . . . You get the picture. And after all that, Barry just used a spell to change the date to the year 3017.

perpetually amused look. Nigel immediately felt comfortable with him; they were roughly the same height. Barry liked him because he covered his total baldness with a ridiculous toupee of curly brown hair. Barry always bonded with people as deluded as he was – and it helped that, compared to Henratty's, his scalp was a veritable Woodstock of follicles.

'Nice to meet you both,' Henratty said, extending a toner-smeared hand. 'Copier broke,' he said, and then to Nigel: 'Would you like a Coke?'

'Yes!' Nigel said, happy to be offered a drink that didn't have some weird magic-inducing additive in it. Everything his mother let him drink tasted like incense.

Walking into Henratty's office, they saw paper everywhere: memoranda, correspondence, photocopies; work-orders, updates, status reports – and even the occasional takeaway menu. Great piles were on his desk, constantly sliding to the floor, where they mingled with more of the same. Stacks sat Barry-high in every corner. A path had been cut between the door and the desk, but this was in constant danger of being swallowed up. Paper hung from bulletin boards and burst from inside groaning filing cabinets. Pieces occasionally fluttered from the top of a stack, pushed by slight currents of air-conditioning. The whole room had the feeling of enemy territory – the paper allowed them to be there, and there was no doubt it could drive them out or crush them utterly, if it so desired.

'Sorry the place is such a mess,' Henratty said. 'The job keeps me very busy. I think there are two chairs over there.' The man pointed to a corner. 'Just dig 'em out.'

Memos! Invoices! Interoffice mail! Nigel had read all about this Muddlenalia, but had never seen it before. He was enchanted. Barry, on the other hand, was bored. The family pictures on Henratty's desk didn't move; the Post-Its didn't swear; the stapler didn't fasten things in six dimensions – how on Earth did he stand it?

After they had taken seats, Henratty asked, 'Barry, how much do you know about the Muddle world?'

'Quite a bit,' Barry said. 'I grew up in it until I was about Nige's age.'

'Then you became a wizard, I presume?' Henratty asked.

'Right.'

'How old are you now, Barry?'

'Thirty-eight as of yesterday.' Next to him, Nigel slurped his drink through a straw; plain old high-fructose corn syrup, caramel colour and carbonation – it was bliss.

'Happy birthday, then. Using our tables, in the past twenty-seven years you alone have been responsible for fifty-four thousand calls to report stolen goods, over six billion pounds in lost property, and at least a score of involuntary commitments to the loony bin.'

'Who, me?' Barry said, smiling.

'And that's just the average magic-user. I think it's pretty obvious that you're anything but average.'

'I don't follow you,' Barry said.

'Few wizards do,' Henratty said. 'It's not your fault – that archaic educational system is to blame. Hogwash was moving in the right direction, but now it's all ghosts and secret passages again.'[11]

[11] After being destroyed by Wagner Bros' overenthusiastic special effects people, Hogwash had been rebuilt as a top-of-the-line, thoroughly modern, ruthlessly rectilinear facility. But soon after the modern school was dedicated, the whole place was discovered to be changing, devolving into the same old pile of weathered granite held together by chilly draughts that it had been for centuries. There was a bit of a scandal – Barry suspected Snipe, of course – but a team of wizard building inspectors soon discovered the cause: a millennium ago when Hogwash had been built, its four founders, Putresca Pufnstuf, Godawfle Grittyfloor, Rotunda Radishgnaw and Spartan Silverfish, had placed a powerful curse on the site. No facility located here would ever be anything but crumbling; they had even found a way to make it rickety, not an easy thing to do with granite. 'We have no idea why they did this,' the report read. 'We suspect it was so no one House would become better than the others. Anyway, it's irreversible.' So gradually the computers and fibre-optic wires disappeared, and the high-tech energy-efficient windows reverted to arrow-slits covered with wavy glass. Even the thick, Scotch-garded carpets disappeared bit by bit, until the students once again

Barry bristled a bit. 'That's the way it's always been. That's the way we like it.' He paused. 'That modern school was so – cold.'

'Surely central heating is better than conjuring up fire left and right?' Henratty said blandly.

'I meant "impersonal". Mr Henratty, if we wizards want to be old-fashioned – if we want to do things our way – that's our business.'

'Unfortunately it isn't,' Henratty said. 'I don't mean to be rude – I understand that yours is not a logical people – but it's simple logic: everything comes from somewhere. If you conjure up a hamburger, it comes from some Muddle's plate.'

Barry was dumbfounded. He'd honestly never thought about it.

'In that case, there's no problem – the diner simply gets another one "on the house". But say you conjure a car – then the outcome is a little more serious.'

'You mean every time I conjure a car, some Muddle's car vanishes?' Barry asked.

'Yes. Most of the time they report it as stolen, and get it replaced. But perhaps they feel they lost it. "What sort of idiot simply loses a car?" their wife might say. That sort of

shuffled across chilly stone. As with most copies, certain slight errors were introduced. It was backwards, for one thing, and Grittyfloor Tower refused to regenerate its roof.

thing can hurt a marriage. Even if the Muddle is an easy-going chap – "Oh, well, easy-come, easy-go" – he or she now lives in a world where cars just disappear. People have been driven insane by less.'

Nigel stopped slurping. 'What if a wizard takes it while they're driving?'

'Road salsa,' Henratty said.

Nigel laughed. 'Ow.' Coke had gone up his nose.

'So you see, the human cost of your magic is incredible,' Henratty said. 'If the general public ever found out that wizards were behind all the mayhem – everything from lost keys to World War Two – they'd wipe you out without a second thought.'

Barry's mouth fell open. 'World War Two? How –?'

'It's a long story. I've got a book if you want to read it.' He plucked a book out of a drawerful of them, and gave it to Barry: *Magic: The Silent Killer*.

'But we don't mean to—' Barry said. 'I mean, we don't know what we're doing.'

'That's where Special Branch comes in – so that nobody else will either,' Henratty said. 'We're trying to conceal the truth, so that you and your kind can stay alive.'

Henratty let that sink in, then said, 'Would you like to have a look around?'

'Yes, please,' Barry said, feeling vaguely nauseated.

'Can I take this with me?' Nigel asked.

'Sure,' Henratty said. 'Hey, is that a Doctor Whom badge on your satchel there?'

'Yes.'

'I liked him too, when I was a lad. Zooming around Time in that portable toilet of his.'

'I have a little replica of the P.O.T.T.Y.[12] on my desk,' Barry said. Nigel gave him a dirty look – this Muddle was *his* special Doctor Whom friend, not Dad's. His dad was always doing that, poaching his friends.

Henratty escorted them to a big, open room, where at least twenty men and women worked in cubicles. Phones rang incessantly. At the far end of the room, there was a map of the world with little red witches' hats blinking on and off.

'This is the Media Control Room,' Henratty said. 'We monitor every Muddle news feed in the world for traces of magical events. Then we disseminate the appropriate counter-information. Take crop circles, for instance.'

'I know who—' Barry was about to say that he knew the two guys who invented those, Ferd and Jorge Measly, but thought better of it.

'Aliens, right? That's what everybody thinks, thanks to us,' Henratty said. 'As if aliens would waste their time

[12] Portable Outerspace Time Travel You-Know-What.

with such nonsense . . . Whenever some wizard idiot decides that the Tube isn't good enough and unrolls a scrap of flying wall-to-wall over central London, we're on the phone to the police instantly saying that we've seen an extraterrestrial. In rare cases, we may even fudge up a videotape.'

'Now, see, we've got that covered,' Barry said. 'The Ministry of Magicity comes over with their Memory Charms . . .'

Henratty gave a harsh little laugh. 'Barry, do you have any idea how many Muddles see your Ministry people going around in their funny outfits, waving their magic sticks? We had to come up with the whole "men in black" legend to compensate. You zap one person with a Charm, but in the meantime twenty more people have seen you guys creeping about acting weird, listening to potatoes and things.'

'Oh,' Barry said, crestfallen.

'I frankly don't know what we'd do if not for those mythical little green men,' Henratty said.

'Aliens are real,' Nigel said. 'My dad saw some.'

'Really,' Henratty said. 'You sure there's nothing funny in that Coke?'

'Yes,' Nigel said, offended. Rhetorical questions flummoxed him.

'He's telling the truth,' Barry said. 'People in my neighbourhood get abducted all the time.'

'Uh-huh,' Henratty said. 'I wouldn't hold my breath, if I were you.'

Nigel piped up, 'Why do people like ETs more than wizards? I mean, why is it any better?'

'We're not sure, but you've never heard of an alien-burning, have you?'

'Nope,' Nigel said, then his Coke gave up the ghost. (It had an afterlife as a burp.) 'May I have another?'

'Sure,' Henratty said. 'Go down the hall and get one out of the staff fridge.'

Nigel sprinted ahead of them, suddenly deeply involved in some sort of imaginary game that required jumping every so often and providing sotto voce narration. Barry turned to Henratty and said, 'Witch-burnings can't hurt us, you know. They drilled that into us at Hogwash.'

'Ever met anybody who lived through one?' Henratty smiled. 'I thought not. Of course that's what they'll tell you. They don't tell you about the insanity, either. Or the sterility.' The two men kept walking.

'So if your job is so important, why is this building so – average?' Barry asked. There wasn't a gargoyle or flying buttress on it.

'You're being kind, it's a dump,' Henratty said, poking at some water-stained ceiling tiles, provoking a small shower of crumbs. 'But this is the Muddle world – no castles for us. The most important decisions get made in the shabbiest places. There are times I wish I were a wizard. Obviously I'm not alone – look at all the people who've read your books.'

'I must say I'm feeling less good about that since I met you,' Barry said.

Nigel returned with another Coke. The first wave of sugar and caffeine was hitting, and he shook and sweated like a junkie.

They passed another door, which had a sign on it: 'Please Be Quiet – Therapy in Progress'.

'Sometimes the situation calls for a personal touch,' Henratty whispered. 'We have fifty therapy chambers in this building alone.'

'Can I put my ear to the door?' Barry was incurably nosy.

'Sure,' Henratty said.

'So your retirement cake disappeared.' Barry heard a patient, modulated voice. 'I bet that made you feel pretty bad.' No, it couldn't be, Barry thought.

'It's something about the thirty-first of July,' another voice said, on the verge of tears. 'Every thirty-first of July I lose things.' It *was*, Barry thought.

'Would you mind if I went in there and gave that Muddle some money? I think my wife might've—'

'Please don't,' Henratty said firmly. 'Actually meeting a wizard after all this trauma – it could be bad. They could snap.'

Further down the hall, they saw another room filled with bankers trying to counter the effect of treasure on Muddle financial markets. 'If just one dragon dies, all that gold and silver gets dumped into the markets at once – that's what happened in 1929, after Bastinado the Unscrupulous slew that ancient Swedish Meatball. Twelve hundred years' worth of treasure, boom. Everything went haywire, stockbrokers started leaping out of buildings . . .'

'Funny, I always thought Bastinado was a hero,' Barry said.

There was another room, filled with small children in robes and pointed hats.

'Are those wizards?' Nigel asked.

'Too young,' Barry said.

'Your dad's right, Nigel. Those are Muddles inspired by J.G. Rollins's books. Their parents brought them here, to be convinced that they aren't Barry, or Ermine. For that reason, I'd ask you not to linger at the window. Seeing the real Barry might send them into a psychotic rage.'

'Weird,' Nigel said.

'It's sad, really. J.G. herself funds our efforts. We're

about ninety-eight per cent successful.' They took a right turn, and ended up at a door that said 'Black Ops'.

'Whoops, wrong turn,' Henratty said.

'Is that where you keep the guns?' Nigel said.

Henratty paused for a second. 'Um . . . yes.'

Barry was appalled. 'What on earth do you need guns for?'

'Come back this way,' Henratty said. 'Not all wizards are as reasonable as you, Barry,' he said, waving to a pretty colleague walking by. 'She's a wereumbrella, would you believe it?' he whispered. 'Family curse. A little moody, but incredibly – ah – useful.' Henratty looked after her longingly. 'What was I saying?'

'You were talking about wizards being unreasonable,' Barry said, wondering how much of the previous paragraph Nigel had understood. He needn't have worried; the boy seemed to be miming some sort of karate move.

'Right. A lot of wizards are crazy. There's a study—'

'HA!' Nigel said. Henratty looked puzzled.

'My son and I were talking about it on the way from Charlbury,' Barry said. 'I told him I didn't believe it.'

'Believe it, all right. A lot of the wizards we deal with are dangerously crazy – the Ministry of Magicity doesn't like it, but occasionally some gnarled old prestidigitator won't listen to reason and we have to take him down.'

'With bullets?' Barry snorted. 'Not likely.'

'Artillery,' Henratty said. 'Whenever you read about an "urban renewal" project – but that's a last resort. Our job here at Special Branch is to help wizards and Muddles live in harmony, not blow people like Bumblemore to bits.' They were back at his office.

'Bumblemore isn't . . .?' The former Headmister had been missing for a while.

'I really can't comment on that individual,' Henratty said firmly. 'Wizards' Protection Programme. Sorry I brought him up – I should've used another example.'

After they had sat down again, Henratty asked, 'So. Do either of you have any questions?'

'Can I—?' Nigel blurted.

'Get another,' Henratty said, glad he wasn't responsible for the kid's dental bills.

'No—I mean, I'll take it, but I was going to ask, can I tell all my friends at school?'

'Nigel's just about to start his first year at Hogwash,' Barry said.

Henratty smiled. 'The big time. I bet you're pretty excited.'

'Not really,' Nigel said.

'He's a little nervous,' Barry said, tousling the boy's hair. Nigel hated that.

'Well, I know a lot of Muddles – pretty much everybody in this building – who would love to be in your shoes, Nigel. We all do this because we love wizards and magic and such – we're just not magical ourselves. I can't even make balloon animals!' Henratty said.

'So can I? Tell them?'

'You'd be helping us out if you did,' Henratty said with a smile. 'Your generation is the one we have to reach. The more young wizards who practise "safe spells", the less trouble we'll have down the road. When in doubt, keep your wand in your pocket, Nigel.'

They all laughed. After another Coke, and a badge that read 'Safe is Super', Barry and Nigel left the building.

'Put on your nose and glasses,' Barry said, handing his son a ridiculous disguise. 'We don't want to be mobbed by paparazzi.' The block was empty.

'Dad, let's take the Tube,' Nigel said.

'Do we have to?' Barry asked. He hated the Tube; the wizard's version was magically connected to every other subway system in the world. This was charming, until you got off at the wrong stop and found yourself in São Paulo. How sodding whimsical, Barry thought angrily the last time it had happened. The whole magical world needed a little less whimsicality and a little more mouthwash, he often said. His battles with the Department of Whimsicality were legion.

'Only if it's the Muddle level,' Barry said. The wizard level was accessed by an electrical box at the end of the

Muddle platform. That way, magical folk could materialise out of the gloom without arousing suspicion. They dressed like homeless people anyway.

After they got on the Tube, Barry looked around and said to his son, 'I think that man was an animagi.'

'Oh, come on, Dad,' Nigel said.

'No, think about it: Hen-ratty – a hen plus a rat. What does that give you?'

'At KFC, a lawsuit,' Nigel said, laughing.

'Go ahead, laugh,' Barry said, mocked by his own child. 'Plus, it's common knowledge that most animagi are asses. The plural of anus is ani. Ani plus magi gives you "magicians who are arseholes". That's Latin, you'll be learning that at school.'

'I thought he was charming,' Nigel said.

'He bribed you with caffeine,' Barry said. 'Get up, this is the stop for Catty Corner.'

Chapter Three

THE OBLIGATORY TRAIN-PLATFORM CHAPTER

One bright September morning about three weeks later two disembodied arms pushed a trolley loaded with belongings down King's Curse famous platform 3.14.[13]

Rubbish – one-time use intoxication scrolls, crisp packets, losing tickets from the Elvish Sweepstakes – piled up in front of the wheels. Occasionally the trolley would stop, and the arms would disappear. Then a disembodied trainer would appear, kicking at the trash to clear it away. A scrawny rat scampered between tracks. 'How could somebody just abandon their familiar like that?' Nigel said to no one. More or less concealed by his father's Cape of Invisibility, he patted the octopus hanging in a bag of brine at his waist. His familiar,

[13] . . . 15926535 . . .

Chesterfield sloshed back cheerily.

A F.X. Potts's Everyscent Novelty Condom – 'For Entertainment Purposes Only' – had wrapped itself around the right front wheel. There was no way Nigel was touching *that*, even with his foot. He pushed the trolley harder and it snapped. Not very durable; luckily there were spells for that. Not that Nigel knew any; whenever Ermine nagged Barry sufficiently to attempt 'The Talk', his father always came away appalled at what Valumart's wizard-specific cable channel, ValuVision, had already taught him.

'It's healthy curiosity,' Nigel's mum said.

'He obviously gets it from his mother,' Barry replied. 'I'm surprised he doesn't have hair on his eyeballs.'

Ermine had launched into a blistering counterattack, the centrepiece of which was Barry's extensive sexual history. Several sordid minutes later, she was only halfway through the Bs when an exasperated Nigel had looked up from his book and said, 'I'm sitting right here, you know.'

'Sorry, Nige,' Ermine said.

'Yeah, sorry,' Barry said.

'Did you know that octopuses are as intelligent as house cats?' Nigel hated it when his parents talked about their lives before they got married. It gave him a creepy feeling somehow. Nigel insisted that his mum put a

Memory Charm on him, so he wouldn't have to think about his parents having sex.

Back on the platform, a centrefold depicting a nyad with an improbable bosom pinwheeled in the breeze. Despite its fame, platform 3.14 had been filthy since the Ministry of Magicity privatised the Hogwash Express (now nicknamed the 'Hogwash Depress'). Since then the journey to Hogwash, which was boring under the best of circumstances, had become a Dantean ordeal of breakdowns and delays, skyrocketing prices and lavatories that reeked of myrrh-tinged pee. The train always left late, but today the Trotters were happy for it – Barry always did, too.

Hogwash was the world's most famous magical school, and Nigel Trotter was its most famous incoming student. He was, after all, the first-born son of Ermine Cringer and Barry Trotter. He had a lot to live up to – a person can cut quite a swathe in eleven years of secondary education, especially someone as extravagantly magical as Barry was. Nigel had heard all the stories, and had no interest in competing. Were it up to him, he would've gone to a Muddle school instead and become a holistic dentist, like his maternal grandparents. But his dad insisted that Nigel at least try Hogwash . . . and so here he was, tussling with prophylactics alongside the peeling, shoddy Hogwash Depress.

The cart lurched as he skidded over a dead gnome. His dad's familiar, Earwig, croaked bitchily with every jolt.

'SKWARK,' the nicotine-stained snowy owl said with a burr of white noise. After years of smoking, she had undergone a tracheotomy, and now hooted through a throat box.

Nigel wasn't carrying his dad's familiar by choice. Not only was it the start of term, it was also Reunion Weekend, which meant that his mum and dad were coming along. (Thankfully, Hurricane Fiona had been fobbed off on Gran and Gramps Cringer.) He was so embarrassed by them that he insisted on walking ahead, and wearing his father's old Cape of Invisibility for good measure. Nigel wasn't looking forward to the trip – it was long and boring; doubly so under the watchful eye of his mother. The rumours of multi-dimensional kissing parties made this particularly bitter. He'd escape somehow. Or, more likely, not.

Twenty feet behind, Nigel's parents bickered lightly. With no Fiona to manage, they had a lot of excess energy.

'What?' Barry said. 'Shiver me timbers . . .'

'I said, "You're insane",' Ermine said.

'I can't hear you, matey, me wig is falling off,' Barry said. Lifting up his eye-patch, he looked at the schedule.

'*Brobdingnag*!' he bellowed, and the schedule got bigger.[14]

'I am *not* a nag!' Ermine said indignantly. 'Hurry, Barry!'

'Relax, landlubber, we still have' – Barry squinted and scanned – 'negative two minutes.'

'Come on, Mum and Dad!' the pair of disembodied arms shouted. 'They're going to leave without us!' Nigel was high-strung.

'Going as fast as I can, matey,' Barry muttered. 'You try walking on one leg.' His hat fell off.

'Leave it,' Ermine said, stopping so Barry could catch up.

'But Erm, the deposit – arr—'

'Leave it,' Ermine commanded.[15] Tagging along behind her was a self-rolling wizard carry-on. Her husband, sweating profusely, caught up.

'Bugger this,' he said breathlessly, taking off the artificial peg-leg. The clown costume would've been a better choice.

'You really should get in better shape,' Ermine said. 'You're sweating like mad.'

[14] Spells were very useful, but they were like dogs – the louder and more sternly you cast them, the more likely they were to pay attention and do what you wanted.

[15] Husbands worked the same way as spells did.

'These inflatable parrots are heavier than they look,' he said acidly.

'I can't understand why you insisted on that stupid costume.'

'Arr, I told you before, it's not a costume, it's a *disguise*,' Barry said, grimacing for effect. 'I can't understand why you wouldn't wear yours. Arr!'

'It was a French maid's outfit!' Ermine said.

'If we get mobbed by paparazzi, it's your fault, matey.' The platform was nearly empty.

Up ahead, Nigel was poking the train with his wand, tap tap. For a magical train, it looked pretty rusty. He examined his wand with some bitterness; poking was at the far end of its powers, probably. It was no thing of beauty, a cheap plywood job he and his dad had picked up last week at Wand Depot. Why waste money on a wand, when the boy behind it wasn't very magical?

As soon as they had stepped into the industrial-strength air-conditioning of Wand Depot, his father had started reminiscing. 'Back when I was a lad,' Barry began, using the universal code for 'stop listening', 'everybody got their wands at Colliemander's. It was run by dogs. You could never find anything – dogs can't alphabetise – but it had charm.' Barry sighed.

'Charm, like magic?' Nigel had asked, finishing off his

Fluke bar. The combination of chocolate and sliminess was strangely compelling.

'I don't think so, but given how often the salesmen humped your leg, maybe.' Barry then remembered the frequency with which customers stepped in poo. 'Actually, almost certainly. They'd stick you with any old piece of crap wand, charge you double, and bite you if you complained. Plus the place was crawling with fleas,' Barry said as they walked down the wide, brightly lit aisles of the Wand Depot.

Nigel had looked around at the warehouse, all exposed ironwork and fluorescent lights, and the glum salespeople in their scratchy, ugly aprons. 'I think I would've liked the old place better,' he said romantically.

'Not me,' Barry said, lying to make himself feel better. As he aged and things changed, inevitably for the worse, he used this technique frequently. 'This is much better,' he said without conviction.

The whole place felt cold and impersonal, and both father and son wanted to get out of there as fast as possible. So, in ten minutes, they had got an oversized plywood chopstick containing a single vole hair. 'It wasn't exactly a magical vole,' the salesman said. 'But it was one quite skilled in, uh, Volery. Try it out.'

Nigel gave it a preliminary swipe, and knocked over a

display of super-light carbon-fibre wands from Denmark. 'It's heavy,' Nigel said.

'It's *durable,*' Barry said. 'You'll get used to it.' They had to get all of Nigel's school supplies bought in one day, so he was in no mood to consider. 'We'll take it.'

'But I — ' Nigel interjected. He wanted one of those L-shaped ones that they always used in the Hong Kong wizard-fu gangster movies. You could shoot around corners.

'Your mum would kill me,' Barry said apologetically. 'Tell you what: pick out a cool holster.' Nigel got one with flames shooting up the sides.

'Do you want training wheels on the wand?' the clerk asked them as they were checking out. The clerk was clearly suffering through the worst summer job of his life, and Barry felt obliged to say yes.

'Dad, n — ' Nigel said.

'Yes, fine,' Barry said. 'You can always take them off,' he said to Nigel.

'Dad! Those are for little kids!' Nigel said. 'Everybody will make fun of me.'

'Well, better for them to make fun of you than to veer during a spell and end up teleported to Sweden when you meant to go to Swindon.'

'I'll use travelling snuff,' Nigel said, in absolute desperation.

'You will not,' Barry said. 'That stuff'll rot your septum away and give you a uni-nostril.' Barry pulled out his G'ingots debit card, and the purchase was made.

That was how Nigel ended up with a wand best suited for rapping knuckles – or poking once-magical conveyances, as the case might be. His parents caught up with him; he had taken off the cape and tied it around his throat like a superhero. This created a disconcerting floating head effect, enough to make a Muddle scream, puke, and pass out in rapid succession – but magical folk were inured to such sights.

Barry took out his wand, and swiped it, mumbling. Nigel's trunk didn't budge.

'Don't hurt yourself, Barry,' Ermine said. 'Cast with your knees, not your back.'

Barry moved the trunk into the waiting bay on the second try. Putting his wand away and wiping the sweat from his upper lip, he turned to his son, who was involved in a bit of fairly intricate play-acting a few feet away.

'Ha! "Delete." Suck it, foul Gasman!' he said, vanquishing a villain with a stroke of an imaginary key.

'Don't say "suck it",' Ermine said.

'Christ, that's heavy, Nigel,' Barry said. 'What do you have in there?'

'Just clothes and stuff.' This was only technically true. Roughly half of the clothes his mother had packed now lay on his bedroom floor, replaced by the rulebooks, character sheets, comptroller's screens and dice for 'Accountants and Attorneys', a Muddle-based role-playing game that he and his mates were mad about. Nigel's daydreams, of which there were plenty, often had him acting out his favourite character, a sixteenth-level, immensely powerful computer systems analyst named Geoff. Nigel had spent the last year building him up from a first-level trainee fresh from university. In Nigel's mind, Geoff had just beaten a fierce meter-reader by hacking into the gas company's customer records. Nigel hoped other Hogwash students played A&A.

With a hiss, the Hogwash Express let out a great cloud of steam. This steam congealed into a conductor who shouted, 'All aboard!' right into Barry's ear. Then added, 'Step lively, Long John.'

'Suck it,' Barry said irritably. Then, worried that somebody might have seen through his disguise, he brandished his plastic sword and growled, 'I'll run you through, you scallywag.' His mood brightened, as he saw someone with a camera striding towards them. 'See?' he said to Ermine triumphantly. The never-ending battle of who was smarter had turned in his favour for the moment.

Only it hadn't. 'Hullo, Barry – Ermine – I'd hoped you'd be coming to the Reunion.' It was Colin Creepy, one of the most disappointing flameouts of Barry's generation. While at Hogwash, Colin had become a legend after introducing Page Three girls to the school newspaper the *Hogwash Haunt*. By his fifth year, he had amassed a sizeable personal fortune and was considering starting his own website, until Bumblemore got wind of what was going on and put a stop to it. Colin was using a charm to have people get naked. Confiscating the photos, the headmister was more rueful than angry. 'If you keep doing stuff like that, you'll have nothing to look forward to, Creepy,' he said. 'Take it from somebody a hundred and forty-two and counting, you'll need all the surprises you can get.'

Unfortunately Colin's first adult surprise was an unpleasant one, in that the *Daily Soothsayer* wasn't interested in yet another bright young Hogwesian. So he fell in with the wrong crowd – the *Stun* – and dropped from there: he had spent the two decades since graduation scraping by in the lowest echelons of wizard porn, dreaming up more and more rococo perversions for Valumart's various skin mags. He was currently editor of *Barely Magical*, *Chesty Enchantresses*, *Hags of Hentai*, and *Succubus Suck-Off*.

As a result, he exuded sleaziness; it hung around him like a fine mist. Colin Creepy was nobody Ermine wanted around Nigel. Barry, predictably, thought Colin was amusing.

The group boarded the train. 'Is this your kid?' Colin asked. 'How'd that happen?' Decades spent fricasseeing in the world of recreational sex had dulled him to its utilitarian aspects. 'Can I sit with you guys?'

Ermine leapt in, with the practised timing of a spouse. 'No, Colin, sorry. We're holding a seat for Lon Measly.'

'Oh.' Colin was a little crestfallen. He'd always wanted to be part of their group at school, and now . . . The déjà vu of the weekend was starting early. 'I understand. I'll find a seat somewhere,' Colin said. He snapped a picture, as he always did when he felt uncomfortable.

Colin caught the look Ermine gave him. 'That's a clothed one – promise.' He turned to Barry. 'Maybe we can catch up over the Reunion. I've got some spectacular shots of the Delphic Orifice.'

'Sounds great,' Barry said. He'd always wanted to go there.

'And I dug up some old caning videos we shot,' Colin said. 'Remember those?'

'Gosh, I don't,' Barry said, blushing. Ermine was watching him like a hawk, one that disapproved of talking about certain subjects in front of small hawks.

'Sure you do!' Colin said. 'You, Imogene Blagg,

Priscilla Tinsly-Thompson and I broke into Bumblemore's office and—'

'Ahem, wife!' Barry said, under a cough.

'Oh, okay. Right,' Colin said. '*We'll talk about it later,*' he said with a wink.

Now he was even starting to weird Barry out. 'Colin, I'll see you at school, okay?'

'Okay,' Colin said, and went engineward; Ermine guided the family in the other direction. They found an empty compartment and sat down.

Nigel opened his backpack, which he'd crammed full of things to make the journey bearable. On top were his five favourite comics – all 'Tales of the Utterly Expected', starring Norman Normal, Middle-Aged Muddle.

The fact was, Nigel didn't like magic, not in the least. It made him nervous – sticks were always turning into snakes. You never knew whether you were about to walk into a normal fog, or a Mambo-Inducing Miasma. Look at some tarted-up waitress the wrong way, and you'd end up having a mass of centipedes where your entrée was supposed to be. Oh, the world of magic was all right if you were natural-born super arsekicker wizards like Mum and Dad – nobody messed with them – but for Nigel it was nerve-racking and thoroughly unpleasant.

'Not everybody who goes to Hogwash wants to be a

wizard,' Barry had said last night, trying to put a good face on it. 'The things you learn are useful in all walks of life.'

'Name one,' Nigel said.

'Don't twist my words around,' Barry snapped. 'You're going to Hogwash, and you're going to like it. That's final.' Nigel had whistled the theme tune to 'Bridge Over the River Kwai' as he finished packing, just to make his feelings absolutely clear.

'I told you we shouldn't let him watch that on ValuVision,' Barry grumbled.

Twelve hours later here they all were, wheezing towards Nigel's future. Ermine got out a magazine of her own. Barry settled in with a quill and pad. He had made a big show about 'starting my memoir' on the train.

Full of energy, Barry wrote: 'Chapter One.' That's a good start, he thought; now what? To give himself a little more time to think, he underlined it twice. Then, to his utter astonishment, like a gift from the Gods of Creation, he thought of something to write.

'I am born,' he wrote.

Now what?

Unfortunately the creative stream, so recently in flood, abruptly ran dry. Doodling did not help. The lines on the parchment were grim and challenging, like thin, stern mouths. Just to show them who was boss, he crossed out 'born' and replaced it with 'bored'.

Disgusted, Barry picked up one of his son's comic books.

'What's this about?' he said, flipping through it, hoping for some good, healthy occultism.

'Well,' Nigel said, instantly warming to his topic, 'it's about a forty-seven-year-old Muddle named Norman Normal, who's an actuary.'

'What's that?' Barry asked.

'He predicts when people are going to die,' Nigel said.

'Oh, he's a banshite,[16] then?'

'No, he uses complex tables. He lives with his mother in Slough. He's got all these cool powers, like probability and statistics—'

'Superstitious nonsense,' Barry said.

'No, it's great. It's a whole different world. One that has a place for *everybody*, not just super wizards – unlike some worlds I might mention,' Nigel said pointedly. 'His big weakness is a tendency to put on weight. Here,' Nigel said, 'look at this one. He goes shopping for milk.'

Barry looked at the brightly coloured cover. 'The one I'm reading is about the small-claims court.'

[16] A gaunt, terrifying spirit with a piercing wail who appears when someone wishes that somebody else in their family would die (or at least leave them the hell alone).

Barry took the other one, looking at them both like they were covered in mucus. He handed them back. Nigel knew what was coming – he'd heard it many times before.

'You know, Nige, one of these days you're going to have to put all this Muddle junk away.'

'Shh, Barry,' his mum said, looking up from her fashion magazine, *Coven*. 'Let Nigel have his fun. He's got enough on his mind.' There was a commotion in the passageway outside as Lon Measly galloped by, chasing a tennis ball. 'Go and collect Lon.'

Barry got up; as he was leaving, he turned to his wife and said, 'We're not helping him by coddling him, Erm. Sooner or later, he's going to have to grow up and be a wizard. Daydreaming's fine when you're a boy, but when you're eleven it's time to start living in the magical world.' Lon galloped past in the other direction. 'Hey, Lon, wait—'

There was a crash followed by swearing and barking and cheers, as Lon upended a refreshments trolley.

Nigel hated it when his dad talked about him like he wasn't there. Even worse, what his dad said fanned the flame of his worry; Nigel had tried hard to keep it small, but it was now a massive blaze, consuming every good feeling he had.

It was just Nigel and his mum in the compartment. As

the train lurched forward, and his father ran back and forth chasing after Lon, Nigel felt a tickle in his throat. He coughed. 'I think I might have the Black Dearth,' he said to his mother. 'If I have the Black Dearth, do I have to go?'

'It's Black *Death*, lamb,' Ermine said, 'and you don't have that.'

Nigel looked out of the window for a bit, in misery. 'Why do I have to be magical?' he said. 'Why can't I just go to a normal school, with normal kids in it? I'm not like you and Dad – I'll never be a great wizard.'

'Don't worry,' she said. 'Nigel, what makes a person great – it's usually a bit of luck, or some special talent even they didn't know they had until they used it. Not everybody can be great, but everybody can be good, and in the end that's just as important.

'You're going to do fine, I know you will.' But in her heart, Ermine was worried too. Hogwash wasn't easy, and children could be terribly cruel. What would happen to her sweet, smart, entirely unmagical son?

Chapter Four

HERE COMES THE DUD

From the day he was born, Nigel Trotter had been magic-free. He couldn't conjure or curse, prestidigitate or levitate. Nigel wasn't clairvoyant – he didn't even have a decent sense of direction. His utter inability to converse with any member of the animal kingdom made trips to the zoo with his dad a drag beyond measure. He was, to put it bluntly, a dud.

Nigel had a keen sense of himself as an utter let down, at least in part because he looked exactly like his father, save for the interrobang. Of course his parents were concerned. His dad blamed his mum's Muddle genes; his mum accused his dad of casting too many spells without protective lead underwear. There was nothing physically wrong with Nigel. Was it a curse? Was it psychosomatic? After ten years of the best doctors (and a few of the worst ones), innumerable painful tests, and a range of therapies and medicines as varied as they were useless, nobody knew for sure why Nigel wasn't magical. His little sister was, preposterously so. A morning didn't go by without Fiona conjuring a warthog, or something else equally disruptive. But his parents would never discipline her.

'Mum, Fi's telling grass snakes to poo in my bed,' Nigel had said recently.

'I *not*!' Fiona said with a spiteful look, setting Nigel's shirt on fire slightly.

'Fiona, stop,' Ermine said, feeding a strip of raw bacon through a glob of blue flame suspended in midair.

'I wish you wouldn't use floating methane, Mum,' Nigel said. 'It makes the bacon taste like farts.' Ermine cooked as though she was furious with the food. Even no-fail spells from Nutella or Mothra Stuart yielded only vaguely organic glop. Barry had taken to calling takeaway food 'an intervention', as in, 'Darling, I think it's time for an intervention.'

Fiona was making the leaves of the kitchen table flap like the wings of an enormous wooden bird. Why didn't his parents stop her? Nigel thought. If I ever did something like that . . .

One of the hinges squeaked. 'Hear that?' Ermine

asked her husband. 'Did we buy this at Wickea? Bloody cheap.'

Barry's newspaper was being thrown up into the air. A butter dish, which Nigel was using to butter his toast, fell to the floor.

'Nigel, why are you so clumsy?' Ermine said, reassembling the broken pieces with a wave of her wand.

'I was just—'

'You know your sister likes to play with the table,' Barry said.

'So it's my fault? We're living with the Exorcist, and I get in trouble?'

'The doctor says it's a completely normal phase. They call it the Terrible Twos,' Ermine said, sitting down and trying to hold the nearest table-leaf down.

'She happens to be three,' Nigel pointed out.

'You did the same thing,' Barry said, leaning with both arms on the table, hoping to keep it from actually taking flight. 'Without the magic, of course.'

'Nigel no magick,' Fiona said. It was one of her favourite themes. 'Noooo magick! Ththpbbb,' she said again, adding a raspberry.

'Ththpbbb,' Nigel did back. He really regretted teaching her how – his smallest attempts to reach out always backfired, like when she told Mum he'd let her lick a slug. She wanted to lick it! He just facilitated it!

'Nigel, stop torturing your sister,' his father said, idly scanning the paper for mentions of his name (which happened less and less these days).

'But I wasn't! She was torturing me,' Nigel said in a voice high with indignation.

'I find that hard to believe, Nige,' Barry said. 'What can a little girl like her do to a big fellow like you?'

'Loads of things! Last night, I woke up and my head was a coconut!'

Barry looked above his glasses at his son. This meant, 'I don't believe you.'

'I put a load of anti-magical salve on it,' Nigel said.

His mother yelped. 'How much did you use? That stuff's expensive!'

'I don't know, a handful?'

'Nigel!'

'Don't get into your mother's medicine cabinet,' Barry said. This had become an issue ever since Nigel had been caught using a douche bag and hose to squirt water out of the second-floor window. It was an honest mistake – how was he to know?

'What's that hair all over you?' Nigel said, changing the subject. Tufts of the stuff were protruding from his father at odd locations.

Barry had recently given in and purchased a bottle of Sir Cedric's Fantastic Follicle Encouraging Emollient, in the hopes that it could arrest his formerly famous mop's inexorable march to the back of his head. ('Strongest stuff I know,' the chemist had said. 'Look – "Now with 25% more YETI!"') He had placed it on the edge of the bath that morning and clumsily knocked it in. Only a few ounces got out, but it was apparently enough to coat him in a fine down, which had, at random intervals, sprouted into something more.

'Nothing, eat your breakfast,' Barry said, smoothing a cowlick on the back of his hand, and turned back to his paper. It was time for Stage Two: drawing caption balloons on every photo, usually filled with rude things. Since it was a wizard paper, the people actually said them. The Muddle Prime Minister suddenly said to a group of prominent women,

There once was a man named St John,
Who was blessed with a whopping great engine.
Whenever his wife
Would fear for her life
St John would scold, 'Stop your wingeing.'

Barry cackled at his mischief as a plate of bacon and eggs floated to a stop in front of him.

'Where's your water bag, Nigel?' Ermine asked.

'Upstairs.'

'Well, it's not making your room more magical. Go and put it on,' his mother said. 'It can't help you if you don't wear it.'

'I don't want to wear it,' Nigel said. 'It looks like a colostomy bag!' This was the latest attempt at upping Nigel's magic quotient. Barry had called Chi Ching, an old school friend now running a feng shui consultancy drive-thru in San Francisco called 'The Happy Hexagram'. She had suggested Nigel have some water on his person. So, all summer, he had a plastic bag filled with water attached to his belt. This was incredibly dorky, especially on the few occasions where it had burst and Nigel had looked like he had suffered catastrophic bladder failure. The only good thing was that before he left for school Nigel was able to pick an octopus as his familiar, and they were cool. Fi was scared of it, which was even cooler.

'Go and put it on,' Barry said to his son, who scowled.

'You might be interested to know that I hate you both!' Nigel stomped off, feeling unappreciated as usual. They were the weirdoes, not him! 'I don't see what's so important about magic,' he fumed. Who needed magic? His bedroom door opened just fine using the doorknob, instead of that stupid incantation Mum spent all last Saturday trying to teach him. Muddles didn't have magic, and they got along well enough. Some day he would escape to the Muddle world! He'd show them!

But first, he had to go to Hogwash. He didn't want to, but his Dad was especially keen on it.

'That school made me the man I am today,' Barry would say.

'Now, Barry, that's never been proved,' his wife quipped.

'Ha, ha,' Barry said. 'Anyway, we're not talking about me, we're talking about Nigel. And it's not just the old school tie, Ermine,' Barry said. 'Can you imagine what people would say if my son—'

'*Our* son,' Ermine chimed in.

'– our son didn't go to Hogwash? For one thing, people would say I didn't like Dorco Malfeasance.' Dorco was the school's Headmister.[17]

'You don't.'

'That's not the point,' Barry said, then sputtered to a

[17] Dorco had suffered a tragic stupidity accident involving the basilisp. Given up for dead, he had been installed as a statue in front of the school. However, a student spilled a mandrake malted drink on him, and Dorco was revived.

stop. What the point was, precisely, was never determined, in this or any other conversation. The only tangible result was that, for better or worse, Nigel was going to Hogwash, and he'd just have to make the best of it.

The trip to Hogwash was as long and boring as ever, and Lon insisted on barking at everybody who walked by the compartment so, as nervous as he was, Nigel was actually happy to see the old pile haul itself into view.

The train stopped. 'Hallelujah,' Barry said, stretching. Lon, who had just fallen into a fitful doze, jumped up and began barking wildly.

'I think he's getting more dog-like as he ages, don't you?' Ermine said, with a shred more affection than Barry cared for. Nigel certainly agreed with her – Lon had just gnawed the head off another action figure, which would eventually come out the other end, the ultimate indignity.

Nigel's parents kissed him goodbye, and went off to board a luxurious touring bus (what J.G. would so charmingly call a 'horseless carriage') that would take them to the school. The bus had been paid for by Lee Jardin, who had become the most famous sportscaster in the wizarding world, despite a ridiculous dreadlock toupee and a well-publicised penchant for wearing women's underwear.

Nigel, on the other hand, went with the other first-years, who were collected by the unkempt giant Hafwid, who, as usual, dispensed profanity and coherence in a ratio of at least four to one. This made him a great favourite, when he wasn't stealing your lunch.

'F'ck'n f'st-yurs,' Hafwid said. 'C'm wi'me.' Though Hafwid was rumoured to have been at many Trotter holiday gatherings when he was a baby, Nigel recognised him instead from the short-lived show 'Hunting with Hafwid'. The show had been cancelled, after it had become too expensive due to all the fines.[18] Nigel and his mates had loved it, though; it was great fun to see how Hafwid got injured this week. Fogged by alcohol, the giant would inevitably get involved in some unspeakably dire situation. Once a Muddle Army battalion was decimated trying to extricate him from

[18] Hafwid cracked the 'f' whip so constantly – using it as a noun, verb, adjective, adverb, and, once, a proposition – that even the most careful bleeping let a few expensive expletives make it on the air. Week after week, month after month, this added up. (Simply to save paper, I am omitting most of Hafwid's profanity, but readers are encouraged to imagine it. A good rule of thumb would be at least two profane intensifiers and one obscene noun stand-in – usually 'Muddlef'ck'r' – per sentence. – MG)

the lair of an Irish Whiskeybreath, and the dragon ended up swallowing him anyway.

'G't in!' The giant gestured to a collection of smelly, rotting boats, some so extravagantly unseaworthy that they were already half-submerged. Lon hopped around, barking excitedly. For this term, Lon was going to replace Hafwid's beloved borehound, Fing (simply Hafwid-ese for 'thing'). Fing had been eaten by some exchange wizards.

The dusk was alive with the sound of various carnivorous fish smacking their lips. Looking at the boats, then at the frothing water, the first-years didn't move. 'I don't think my parents . . .' began a weedy little boy named Bertie Pillock.

'I knew yer pa, an' if yer haff as worthlus a wanker as he wus, drownin'll be a favour to yeh,' Hafwid said. 'Get in, you miserable tit!'

Strangely, this didn't reassure anybody.

'Whutter yeh touch-holes waitin' fer?' Hafwid said. 'An engrave invitashun?' He pulled out his flowery pink umbrella and fired several rounds into the air. Then he unscrewed the handle and took a slug.

'MOVE YER ARSES!' Hafwid bellowed, wiping his mouth messily on his sleeve. He was in no mood to be trifled with – he'd spent the past several hours at the

Ho's Head pub in Hogsbleede, drinking and losing heavily at solitaire.

Several students dutifully got in and became Unhappy Meals. 'Whoo jes' died? Ennybody ketch their names?' Hafwid marked down the names of the lost, to notify their families. Nigel's boat was better – a band of merpunks tried to capsise it, until Hafwid paddled over and threatened to 'tear ev'ry wunna yeh a new blow-hol'.

Upon landfall, the first-years were herded into the Great Hall. They were a pitiful sight, shivering in their soaked robes, huddled together at the head of the room. Nor did they smell very good – wet wool, the stink of fear, and the noisy evacuations of many terrified familiars created an incredible pong.

The Great Hall was just as Nigel's parents had described it: floating candles, trick ceiling, long tables crammed with students elbowing each other and bickering. At the foot of every table, ostracised students sat glumly, reading books and ignoring the insults and hot wax tipped on to them by bullies. Will I be one of those? Nigel wondered. Right then he decided: if I am to be an outcast, I'll at least take a bunch of them with me.

The rest of the school banged on the tables and catcalled as the first-years stood there, waiting to be sorted into Houses. The second-years, with last year's humiliations still fresh, were particularly vicious, lobbing rotten fruit at the terrified newcomers. The alumni, who were starting their weekend by watching the Picking ceremony, were at the far end of the room, opposite the newcomers. They had been sitting there for twenty minutes; travel by road was much quicker – the trouser-fouling trip across Lake Eerie was far more a means of hazing than transportation.

Ermine noticed the fruit and was casting a Blocking Spell, but Barry stopped her.

'We shouldn't interfere,' Barry said. 'Nigel wouldn't want us to.'

'But this didn't happen when we were here,' Ermine said. 'It's barbaric. I blame those goddamned Malfeasances.'

'He's going to have to learn to defend himself sooner or later,' Barry said.

Ermine said something unintelligible, but probably not kind.

'What?' Barry said.

'I said, "Wonder where Headmister Malfeasance is,"' she lied.

The High Table was already filled with teachers, save for the large chair in the middle which belonged to Dorco. Most of them had taught Nigel's parents: Snipe was there, looking as malevolent as ever. He had returned to Hogwash after he realised no other job would allow him to beat his underlings. And Hafwid, too, of course – already asleep or passed out or dead, Barry couldn't tell. There was Madame Ponce, the school's librarian of uncertain gender; Professor Bunns, who cut holes in his robes so that his ghostly buttocks were constantly on view; Madame Coochie, the Quiddit instructor with a weakness for jock-sniffing; and chatting Coochie up, Zed Grimfood, the school's Armourer.[19] In the next two seats, swinging wildly and knocking over glassware, were Head Trustee Ludicrous Malfeasance, and Professor Author Measly. Lon's father had retired from the Ministry and was now teaching Muddle Appreciation to the students.[20]

The Hogwash job was far from the biggest change in

[19] It's true, most schools do not have an armourer. But attending Hogwash was fairly dangerous. The staff room had a sign in it that read, '_ Days Without a Dead Student'. It never broke double figures. But a Hogwash diploma opened a lot of doors in the wizarding world, so parents continued to offer up their youngsters like sacrificial lambs.

[20] Former Grittyfloor Headmistress Minolta McGoogle had died. It was very tragic; rambling around the school in cat form, as she often did, Mrs McGoogle had caught, and then choked upon, an immortal mouse. Stuffed in cat form, she now slumbered for ever on the mantel of the Grittyfloor Common Room.

Professor Measly's life; after their last child, Genny, left the nest, the fragile bond of matrimony holding Muley Measly to her balding and befuddled husband was broken. Without so much as a *Divorce-Divvier* incantation, Muley left Lon's father and shacked up with Girlrboy Rockhard. To the surprise of everybody concerned, Professor Measly greeted this news with delight. Apparently he had always felt ill-placed in his body and, for that matter, sexuality. Before his wife had even left the postcode, Professor Measly had transformed himself into a tall, elegant, uncompromisingly gay black man with a blinding white afro. It threw his brood for a loop, but he seemed much happier now.

The only new face at the Table was – as always – the school's Dork Arts and Crafts professor. A visiting professor from somewhere nobody had ever heard of, the man was strange-looking, even in the wizarding world, where rubbing oatmeal into your hair was considered the height of fashion. His face was completely covered with a balaclava of bottle-green wool, with a luxuriant white beard rolling out of the bottom; a pair of half-moon glasses were fixed into position by two scraps of duct tape over his ears.

'He looks familiar somehow,' Ermine said to Barry.

'You know what they say: every wizard looks alike,' he replied. It was true. Years of traffic with powerful magic tended to dry out the hair, wrinkle the skin and twist the features into a characteristic wince. Wizards called it the 'bracing for an explosion' look.

At the head of each table full of students were Hogwash's ghosts: there was Grittyfloor's Barely Brainless Bill, and sitting next to him the Whaling Widow. She was bickering loudly with the Bloody Imbecile, Silverfish's spectral mascot, who was covered with fresh silver blood after gashing his thigh with a chainsaw.

'Bloody Imbecile!' the Widow said. 'Should'a let Hafwid cut that tree down.'

'Shut your blowhole, you briny trollop!' the Imbecile yelled. He pointed. 'Thar she blows!'

The Widow whirled around. 'Where?'

'Made you look,' the Bloody Imbecile said.

'Sit on my harpoon,' she growled.

Back with the alumni, Ermine asked, 'Do you see the Fat Fryer?'

'I can't see anything,' Barry said, strengthening the prescription on his glasses with a snap of his fingers.

'Maybe Filth finally caught him,' Ermine said. Angus Filth was the school's caretaker, and did not care for the greasy schmaltz that the Fat Fryer trailed wherever it went.

'A lot of people have shown up for the Reunion,' Barry said.

'If Dorco's here, then Millicent Belltoad can't be too far behind,' Ermine said.

'Millicent who? All these upper-class names run together,' Barry admitted.

'You remember Belltoad,' Ermine said. 'Amphibian, common to the Western US, with a tail-like copulatory organ. She was in Silverfish.'

'Oh her,' Barry said. 'I hope she doesn't come. She used to beat up all the Grittyfloor boys who hadn't reached puberty yet. Look, there's Lara Madly.'

'I remember her,' Ermine said. 'She was the biggest unitard[21] in Pufnstuf. Wow!'

'What?' Barry asked.

'Creedence Clearwater made it,' Ermine said, pointing at a jangly woman sporting a bowl haircut. 'Prissy Measly's squeezebox.'

'Remember that time she got petrified by the basilisp?' Barry asked with a smile.

'Yeah,' Ermine said. 'Did wonders for her saggy bosom.'

'Meow,' Barry said. Ermine had an unacknowledged thing for Prissy Measly.

[21] A unitard is someone with an excessive love of unicorns.

'What are you guys laughing about?' Hanna Rabbot asked. She was an animagus – her pink nose and floppy grey pigtails gave her away.

'Nothing, Hanna.' Barry liked her well enough, but he couldn't help thinking of rabbit stew whenever he saw her. 'Hi Catie,' he said, waving to Catie Bell and the Drells, her omnipresent backup group. Catie and the four black guys in matching outfits smiled and waved back.

Even a few ghosts had made it for the Reunion. 'Look,' Hanna said, pointing. 'There's that Bones girl who got jumped by Earth Eaters.'

'It's just like old times,' Barry said nostalgically.

So that the Hall would be stuffed to capacity, there was a full complement of Muddles in the glassed-in galleries above. Each September, Muddle hotels nearby featured special cheap rates to encourage Barry Trotter fans to come and see the Picking ceremony. Once word got out that Barry, Ermine and Nigel were going to be there bookings shot through the roof. Clearly, if the structure hadn't been held up by magic it would've collapsed immediately, crushing a third of Pufnstuf House. Ho hum.

Though Nigel tried to make himself inconspicuous, the returning students acknowledged their new celebrity by giving him more than his fair share of abuse. Nigel ducked to avoid a rotten turnip whizzing towards him – being magical, it evaporated, leaving only a whiff of stench. Chesterfield changed colours and shook all eight fists inside his plastic bag. Occasionally a missile would hit one of the candles magically floating in the air, and it would spin end over end, round and round. Would something like that ever stop? Nigel wondered. As he wondered, a furry, definitely non-magical cherry tomato – easily concealable and obviously saved up over the summer for just this occasion – smacked into his cheek, spattering him with foul juice.

A boy standing next to him laughed heartily. He was a very pale, grey-eyed character with a pointed face. Nigel knew that face, knew it from his dad's old school photos. Nigel always paid attention to the ones with this guy in them, because usually something funny was happening. 'Here's us, right after making a porcupine come out of Dorco's urethra,' his dad had chuckled. 'Oh, and here's when Ron used a Marine Epoxy Draught to fix Dorco to his mop! It seeped through his pants and burned holy hell out of his arse!'

'Barry, stop – you're giving Nigel ideas,' his mother had said.

'I'm sure Nigel knows never to do this kind of thing

to anybody,' Barry said. 'Never, ever, ever,' he repeated, silently nodding his head 'yes.'

Actually, Nigel suspected that they would be relieved if he used magic in any way, cruel or not. But Dorco was Headmister. Who was this boy who looked just like him?

'Nice catch, Trotter,' the boy said, as Nigel wiped his head with his sleeve. 'So you're old Scat-Head's son, eh?'

'Are you a janitor here?' Nigel said. 'I didn't see you come over on the boats.'

'I *live* here, wee wand. My dad's Headmister.' He packed more arrogance into this single fact than Nigel had ever thought possible. 'You'll be in Grittyfloor, I suppose?'

'Yeah—' Nigel remembered what his mum had instructed him to say: 'I mean, I'd be happy to go wherever the Picking Cap puts me.'

'Nah, you look like Grittyfloor material to me,' the Malfeasance boy said. 'All the losers are put in there, my dad makes sure.' Since Malfeasance became Headmister, the Cap had been under strict orders to put all the dullest students, the ones that were non-magical, or stupid, or both, into Grittyfloor. (Luckily for Grittyfloor, a lifetime of being sozzled had made the Cap more and more imprecise, and as the process went on it took little nips from a flask hidden in its band. So by the end of the alphabet, the Cap was singing filthy songs and sorting people randomly.)

'Hey, shaddup!' a newly–awake Hafwid yelled, aiming his umbrella to dispense some discipline. He pulled it back once he saw who the offender was. 'Oh, sorry Larval.'

'See, Trotter?' Larval whispered. 'Things've changed since your dad's day. We Malfeasances are running things now.' Larval smirked, then his eye was caught by something up above. Within the inky blackness of the ceiling, among the stars that had been arranged, for a small fee, to read, 'Drink Rhutastic', something was moving. As Larval looked up, rapt, Nigel leaned over and let a gob of spit fall silently from his mouth on to Larval's shoe. The torch of hostility had been officially passed to a new generation.

It seemed like they waited for ever, while Dorco powdered his nose somewhere. The Picking Cap drank, first slyly, then more brazenly with every slug. Students had to send the house elves back again and again for more rotten vegetables. Yet Dorco's seat was still empty. Already beginning to slur, the Picking Cap warbled:

If you don't like the House I pick,
You know what you can do with it.
The quality of applicants makes me sick
I'd rather stock a zoo with it.

Snobs and slobs, Silverfishers are both
Pufnstuffians are ruffians, and angry.
The breath of a Radishgnaw could stunt your growth
A Grittyfloor and a sloth are consanguinary.

A few people listening booed the rhyme. The Picking Cap flipped them off with its floppy peak. 'What do you expect? Shakespeare? I'm a bleedin' piece of headgear!'

Greasy, stringy, crawling with lice,
Your heads are the sum of my fears,
If you want to keep them, here's some advice –
Start grovelling when Dorco appears!

Nigel patted his octopus, who turned pink with pleasure. 'Cool,' a few kids said, then were shushed. Suddenly the doors opened and two house elves traipsed out; each toddler-sized, goggle-eyed kipper was dressed like a Hogsbleede showgirl. Nigel was happy to see them – the hail of trash now shifted targets, pelting the elves as they scattered rose petals.

Two more house elves gave their long metal horns a

prodigious blat. There was a collective gasp as, above them all, something heaved into view. Something large. The rain of produce stopped, and the catcalls shut off as if somebody had turned a spigot.

The flatulising of the horns grew louder, and was joined by the boom of a drum. Nigel could just see in the gloom of the entrance one elf swinging a particularly small comrade by his feet into an enormous bass drum. Having seen this, Nigel winced whenever he heard the beat.

The shadow descended, slowly becoming distinct. Suddenly everybody feared for their lives: there, perched on a crescent of silver foil, was a large man. A *huge* man, swaddled in a toga and strumming a lyre. It was the Headmister. 'Students! Teachers! Alumni! I come to you from the Heavens! The embodiment of Apollo . . .'

Nigel realised just how insane a lifetime of exposure to magic could make you. 'Jesus,' he said under his breath.

'"Headmister" will do,' Larval hissed from behind him.

The years had not been kind to Dorco Malfeasance. His white hair had vanished long ago, save for a posterior fringe that he wore unwholesomely long. Was this balding, and his lack of teeth, and the facial scabs which took so long to conceal with makeup, side-effects of the powerful Dork magic he had used throughout his twenties? (He needed it to get a date.) Only Nurse Pommefritte knew for sure, but what was beyond dispute were the brutal effects that this same magic had wreaked on his organs of procreation, which were roughly the size of raisins and just as effective. Dorco's loins were a blasted heath, yet the ancient and annoying Malfeasance line had to continue (in this book, villains and foils are born, not made). Therefore Ludicrous Malfeasance, a leading Dork wizard and the school's Head Trustee, had arranged for a clone: Larval.[22]

However, some effects of 'the conjuror's comeuppance' (as magi-castration was called in polite company) are not so easily circumvented; Dorco had ballooned preposterously in the twenty Septembers since graduating from Hogwash. Each year's layer of fat formed a base for an even larger one in the year to come. And yet Dorco was not jolly – just the opposite. He ran Hogwash with an iron whim, and though he did not actually kill students, one could see that it was something he aspired to.

Dorco continued to ride his spell downwards, as if an elephant were being lowered, slowly and with inept

[22] However, I'd like to point out that 'I Am Lord Valumart' can be rearranged to spell 'I'd Rut A Larval Mom.' Makes you think, doesn't it?

musical accompaniment, by a silent and invisible crane. All eyes were turned upward; all mouths hung open; the new foreign professor mumbled a prayer in his native tongue. The crowd was transfixed – not by the impressiveness of the event, as much as by the certainty that, were this jiggling orca of a man to fall, at least one and probably more people would be crushed, with extreme messiness and no hope for survival. There were at least thirty stones worth of Dorco under that toga.

And that's exactly what happened. Dorco suddenly toppled, swiped, missed, and fell. Students scattered, but an unlucky house elf was sprayed everywhere. Nigel wiped his speckled specs; it was a gruesome sight – the Headmister wasn't wearing any underpants.

The Muddle fans in the galleries above erupted into applause, thinking that this was an annual thing, some incomprehensible but spectacular tradition. When they realised the big man in the bedsheet wasn't moving, it trickled away. There were a few hastily suppressed laughs, and they were ushered out.

'Oh, no! Genetic material donor!' Larval shouted in grief, right in Nigel's ear.

'Ow! Shit!' Nigel said, as Larval pushed to the front of the group and started to bawl. Nigel didn't understand what Larval was so concerned about. If his parents died, he'd have a great time. He'd write a book about it, take the money and open up a combination dentist's office/A&A parlour.

Nurse Pommefritte rushed over to Dorco, crumpled on the flagstones like a squashed cupcake. His crimson filling – and the house elf's – was oozing all over the flagstones.

'Clean up in Great Hall,' a house elf said over the loudspeaker.

'He's dead,' Nurse Pommefritte said.

'She's right,' the ghost of Dorco said, appearing next to her. 'Let's eat.' Death had not affected his appetite.

Nurse Pommefritte waved her wand, and whisked the drippy corpses off to the School Morgue. Everyone else sat down to dinner.

Severe Snipe filled in to preside over the feast, but no mortals had much appetite, especially those who were showered with flecks of Dorco when the house elves brought out the high-pressure hoses. The elves were positively bouncy after the Headmister's demise. Being asked to row Dorco's pleasure barge was one thing, they enjoyed that in their masochistic way; but being unwilling fuel for its boilers – without an increase in pay! – had offended them.

For their part, the students were subdued. Those who had forgotten Hogwash's lethality after a summer spent in safer circumstances remembered the grim reality. Moaning and throwing up buttons, the Picking Cap was judged to be drunk and put away; and the first-years were simply sorted according to their scores on the Magical Aptitude Test. The most talented were put in Silverfish, the next in Radishgnaw, then Pufnstuf. The others – the dregs – were dumped into Grittyfloor. There was no doubt where Nigel would end up.

The air of the Great Hall was percolating with post-prandial belching competitions – House versus House, students versus alumni – as Snipe stood up and motioned for quiet.

'I'd like to welcome you back to Hogwash where, as we all know, horrible things happen all the time,' Snipe began, and Barry could swear that the Notions professor looked at him; true, the school had become incredibly lethal since he had enrolled. 'Before you go to your rooms to discuss who might be responsible for this incredibly tragic and untimely death' – he nodded to Dorco – 'who might be the next to die, and set a million idiotic plans in motion' – Snipe definitely looked at Barry this time – 'I have a few announcements I'd like to make. First, please join me in welcoming our new Dork Arts and Crafts instructor, Professor . . . '

Snipe leaned over and the odd man whispered something into his ear. 'Speak up, I didn't quite catch that ... Professor Mumblemumble.' Snipe shrugged and made a face like, 'Strange name, but that's what I heard.'

The crowd clapped, and only a few scattered volleys of food were launched, a sign of great respect. The professor conjured a business card and gave it to Snipe.

'Professor Mumblemumble is currently the I.M. Bogus Professor of Wizardry at Ersatz University, it says here. I am sure that he will be a tremendous addition to our faculty this term, as well as important to the plot. Let's all try to make him feel welcome, *not* like one of the family.' Snipe distributed a glare more or less evenly about the room.

'Second, ten points from Grittyfloor, just because I feel like it.' The other Houses cheered. A bell clanged, and the numbers on the lighted tote-board hanging at one end of the Great Hall flipped, and the Grittyflavians fell a thousand points behind their nearest rival.

'I bet he gets airline miles every time he does that,' Barry said. Ermine shushed him. 'Why?' Barry said. 'It's Snipe, for Circe's sake.'

'But he's Headmister for the moment, and we should respect him,' Ermine said.

'I'd remind you that it was you who was responsible

for getting him on the Enchanted-Sex-Toy-of-the-Month Club all those years ago.'

'Shh!' Ermine said. Indeed she had, and thanks to an obscure *Telemarketus* spell that she had dug up in the Restricted Section of the Library, Snipe had been unable to remove himself from the mailing list ever since. His office was full of carnal apparati, crawling all over each other, squelching and purring; just going in there made your orifices twinge.

Snipe was winding up. 'Let's hope this was simply a bad beginning to an otherwise excellent year for Silverfish, and an adequate one for everybody else. Now, Perfects may lead the Houses to their Common Rooms, where they will watch a short orientation film before bed. Goodnight – and may God protect you.'

Chapter Five

ATTORNEYS AND ACCOUNTANTS

Nigel walked with the rest of Grittyfloor to the portrait of the Thin Lady with the Suspiciously Fat Face. This picture's reaction to celebrity was immediate liposuction, which she was paying for by selling peeks up her skirt to curious first-years. She kept auditioning for roles on the sets of Hollywood movies, but never got them – she always waved at the camera.

'Coming through, pigment-puss,' Passé Measly announced haughtily. The Grittyfloor Perfect, he was the son of Prissy and just as annoying. Nigel remembered his dad saying that Prissy acted like he had a wand up his arse; now he knew what Dad meant. Passé wasn't very magical – he was sorted into Grittyfloor – but what he lacked in talent he made up for in self-regard.

'Toll of one Sickie,' the portrait announced. She had lipo bills to pay.

'What?' Passé spluttered. 'That's outrageous! Do you realise who you are talking to? I shall tell the Headmister!'

'Go ahead – he gets half,' the portrait said.

The toll was paid, and the tired, overstimulated students climbed through to the Grittyfloor Common Room. There the room assignments were posted. Nigel knew one name out of the four assigned with him – Don Tomas.

'Everybody find a spot,' Passé yelled. A wand was aimed at a patch of blank wall, and the orientation video began.

The school that awaited Nigel was very different from the one Barry, Ermine, Lon and the others had attended. Decades of being world famous had turned Hogwash, the tumbledown shitpile where you went to learn magic, into HOGWASH, the place to become the next Barry Trotter, wealthy world-saving wizard beloved by billions. Students were so enthralled by the mythology that each one would silently declare him/herself a Barry, or an Ermine, or a Lon; and these atoms would connect with each other in molecules of three. Each student would then roleplay for their entire career, the Ermines studying hard, the Barrys causing trouble, and the Lons being doggish, the three occasionally springing into action to scour the school for 'mysteries' inevitably of the most contrived and infantile sort.

This constant hunting for imagined plots not only gave the school an absurdly high fatality rate, but parents were also required to sign papers waiving any right to sue if 'your son or daughter dies in the course of miscellaneous mystery-solving behaviour, including but not limited to snooping, spying, finding "clues" or misinterpreting same, confronting dangerous animals, antagonising not-so-dangerous animals, rummaging, escaping, exploring, or bothering Professor Snipe'. The staff referred to this behaviour as 'Rollinsitis', and after the hundredth death (a third-year Barry starved after becoming stuck in a heating vent – the Ermine was afraid to tell and the Lon forgot), the chagrined author gave a million Gallons yearly towards its prevention.

Rollinsitis made the actual running of the school – an already thankless task suffered by the house elves – nearly impossible. Though no magical folk would have left their cocoon of self-importance long enough to realise it, they were sitting on a time bomb; the house elves were continually quivering on the edge of a massive walk-out, probably followed by a protracted riot. But as far as anybody with normal-sized eyeballs knew, all was well and the Hogwesian gravy train was still on schedule.

The school's self-regard was evident in the orientation video (a Measly-era innovation, recently updated). The little film, narcissistic under any circumstances, was downright creepy since it was hosted by Dorco Malfeasance, the man who had just plopped to his death before their eyes.

Naturally the students concentrated instead on the elements that played to their vanity – the pageant-like music, the dramatically lit shots of the school looking better than it ever did in real life, the pompous narration emphasising their specialness and the almost unbearable promise of their collective future . . . And thus the process of becoming a Hogwesian began in earnest, that subtle alchemy that, throughout the width and breadth of the wizarding world, made the words 'Hogwash student' synonymous with 'stuck-up arsehole'.

Nigel, being his mother's son, took notes during the film. As he was also his father's son, he got bored halfway through and stopped. Some highlights were:

1) Always comport yourself like wizard — NO TUBE-TOPS/CUT-OFFS.

2) Pretend house elves don't exist.

   a. Browbeat

   b. Ridicule

c. Hit

d. Eat (if necessary or convenient)

3) Don't worry about where conjured stuff comes from.

a. Not your prob (yeah right!)

4) Think of Muddles as ...

a. children→always patronise (use *Patronise* spell)

b. retards→never admit this

5) <u>ALWAYS</u> fob menial activities off on others.

a. Avoid physical exertion at all costs: scrawniness = health.

6) World is two groups: magical/non-magical.

a. like shepherd and sheep

i. sheep provide wool, meat, cuteness

ii. shepherd provides correction when sheep get out of line

Baa, baa, Nigel thought glumly, after the lights came back up. The boys went to their assigned rooms and started to unpack.

Nigel's roommates didn't seem to be suffering from the same worries. There were two Muddle-born boys from the same town, Gordon and Peter, who were already friends[23]. They had scads of inside jokes and pushed each other a lot. They even looked related. Clearly they were a self-sufficient duo, and even if they hadn't been Nigel harboured grave doubts that he could withstand the physical punishment that seemed to come with being their pal.

Next was a kid named Byron. Though there isn't any hard and fast rule saying, 'Don't be friends with an eleven-year-old who wears a cape', there might as well be. His familiar was a peacock named Shelley who crapped all over the place and randomly let out earsplitting screeches.

'I've had sex with my sister,' were Byron's first words to his new roommates. 'And tasted of human flesh.' He waited for this to have an effect. It didn't.

'Nice cape!' Gordon mocked. 'Where are *you* from?'

'Penisland, probably,' Peter said, elbowing his mate.

'Or Willyville!' Gordon said, with a guffaw and a shove.

'Or Choadania!' Peter said, grabbing Gordon's sweater.

[23] Their mothers, clearly not grasping the concept of a familiar, had provided them each with a bag of frozen peas. Gordon and Peter tried to brazen it out by giving them names, carrying them to classes, et cetera, but by Christmas they both had those Sony robot dogs.

Here's my chance, Nigel thought! 'Or, uh—' His roommates looked at him. '. . . Peepeeistan?' Nobody laughed, and Nigel had clearly been placed at the bottom of the totem pole, below Byron and his fourth roommate, Don Tomas. Don wore dreadlocks, like his father, but was named after his *other* father. ('Best friends,' *right* – Don Tomas and Lee Jardin were a lot closer than J.G. Rollins let on.)

Nigel noticed something weird about Don's hair. 'They're not real dreads,' Don confided. 'These cloning spells, they're not a hundred per cent effective.' His hair naturally sprouted in big, thick rolls.

'Does it hurt?' Nigel asked. 'I think it's cool, Don.'

'Thanks,' Don said. 'Call me Junior, everybody does.' His hair, plus his odd name, plus his parentage (one of the first same-sex marriages in the magical community), plus the fact that his familiar was a goat, made him a teaser's delight. He and Nigel bonded immediately – ostracism shared was ostracism halved.

Everybody unpacked their trunks. Gordon had a large CD player in his, while Peter had a large scrying ball, the magical world's equivalent to television. They had clearly planned this beforehand.[24]

[24] The powerful radiation associated with magic initially made Muddle technology and magical folk a bad combination. However, after the Trotter-detente between the races, Lord Valumart set his

'If anybody wants to watch the ball,' Peter said, 'the charge is one Sickie.'

'Per hour,' Gordon said.

'Yeah!' Peter agreed. They high-fived.

'Same goes for the CD player,' Gordon said. 'And if we want to use it, we can kick you off.'

'Yeah!' Peter agreed. They bumped chests.

Independently, each of the other three boys silently made a mental note: break their stuff.

Nigel took out his school books, and piled them on the bed. *Boring and Pointless Spells for Beginners*; *Frigging With the Future*; *Hogwash: A History* ('with clues to the latest mystery in RED!'); *Famous Monsters and How to Prepare Them*; and *The Crooked Book of Crooks*.

'What's that?' Don said, pointing at Nigel's A&A stuff.

'It's a game,' Nigel said. 'It's called "Accountants and Attorneys". You pretend to be Muddles, and solve mysteries and fight bureaucrats and things.' He handed him a set of comptroller's screens, which were covered in pay scales, tax tables, and such.

'Sounds cool,' Don said. 'What's a bureaucrat?'

scientists on to solving this problem. Where there is a will – nourished by enough greed – there's a way, and so now, unlike in Barry's day, there were plenty of CD players, for example, that wouldn't skip if you cast a spell near them.

'It's a kind of Muddle monster,' Nigel said. 'I can teach you how to play later.'

'I *knew* you were an A&A geek,' Gordon said. 'Pay up!' he said to Peter, and Peter handed over some money.

'So you're Barry Trotter's son,' Byron said, stuffing his blood-red, velvet footie pyjamas into a drawer. 'I thought you'd be cooler.'

'Thanks,' Nigel said, wanting to preserve good relations.

'Is it true your dad knows Art Valumord?' he asked.

'Yeah.' Nigel had been sworn to secrecy by Uncle Terry. Being known as a ruthless businessman would kill VTA's thriving second life as a nostalgia band.

'Do you think you could get me his autograph?'

Nigel immediately thought of the likely one scar/one autograph proposition. 'I don't think so,' he said.

'Jerk,' Byron said. When Nigel and Don went to wash for bed, Byron walked over to Nigel's schoolbooks and tore pages out at random. (He 'did over' every single one except for *The Crooked Book of Crooks*. As soon as he touched that one, it immediately pulled out a gun and robbed him.) Peter and Gordon stood there snickering.

When he and Don returned and saw what had been

done, Nigel was livid. Now Nigel would have to buy used copies, and those could be haunted.

'Who did this?' Nigel shouted. The other three boys were silent, until Byron spoke up.

'What do you care? Your dad's loaded, you can afford new ones.'

Being thought rich was a Trotter family curse; nobody knew about Uncle Serious, who had once bankrupted thirteen people with a single business plan.

'Thanks for admitting it, Byron,' Nigel said. The two boys glared at each other; picking up on his master's mood, Chesterfield's mantle was mottled with rage. The bad feelings were still there when they all went to bed.

On a warm night like this one, having no roof on the Tower wasn't a big inconvenience. It was draughty, but between the curtains on the four-poster bed and flannel pyjama-wearing fire salamanders the house elves had slipped between the sheets earlier in the evening, Nigel's bed was cosy indeed.

'You don't have to take that,' Junior whispered to Nigel as the rest of the boys slept.

'I don't want to fight him,' Nigel said. 'He's bigger than I am.'

'So use a spell,' Junior said. 'Knowing who your parents are, I think he'd poop in his robes as soon as you pointed your wand.'

'Well I – I'm not very magical either,' Nigel admitted. 'Don't tell anybody, okay?'

'You probably haven't hit puberty yet,' Junior said, trying to make Nigel feel better. 'Here, I was planning to save these, but take 'em.' He handed him a packet of earwigs. 'I got these in Hogsbleede,' Junior said.

'You went to Hogsbleede?' Nigel said. 'My dad never takes me to Hogsbleede.'

'Dad was announcing a boxing match,' Junior said. 'And other Dad likes Siegfried and Roy. I go there a lot. Anyway, here's what you do . . .' He whispered into Nigel's ear.

'Cool!' Nigel said quietly. 'They'll eat his brain?'

'If he has one,' Junior whispered back.

'Okay, I'm going to do it. Watch!' Nigel said. He slipped on the Cape of Invisibility, and tiptoed over to Byron's bed. Taking out the envelope, he sprinkled a few of the bugs on Byron's pillow. To his delight – and horror – the bugs rose up on their hind legs, sniffed the air, then made a beeline for Byron's ear. One, two, three, disappeared inside. Nigel scurried back to his bed, giggling. Junior was laughing too.

'Would you guys SHUT UP!' Peter or Gordon said, waking up Byron, who scratched his ear, and rolled over.

'Shut up yourself!' Junior said back.

'If it works, maybe we'll do Prat One and Prat Two next,' Nigel whispered.

'Yeah!' Junior said. The co-conspirators laughed into their pillows. It felt good not to be pushed around.

'So,' Junior said quietly, 'do you think your dad did it?'

'Did what?' Nigel responded.

'Killed Headmister Malfeasance.'

Nigel suddenly realised how useful it could be if everybody thought Barry was a killer. 'Maybe,' Nigel said. 'It's the sort of thing he might do.'

'That's hardcore. My dad told me all kinds of stories about him. Seems like a real psycho,' Junior said, then added, 'In a good way, of course. Did he really charm a bottle rocket so that it would zoom up Snipe's bum?'

'That's what he says,' Nigel said. 'I don't know if I believe him, though. Sounds like the Measlys.'

Junior was quiet for a second, then said, 'I bet it's really hard to have him be your dad. I mean, what could *you* do to Snipe for an encore?'

'Tell me about it,' Nigel said. 'I mean, not only does everybody assume I'm going to be this big wizard, it's like he can't be back in school for an hour without somebody dying.'

Nigel didn't fall asleep until one in the morning, what

with the Headmister kicking the cauldron right in front of him, and his nervousness about being at Hogwash and everything. Luckily the first class wasn't until noon – the alumni weekend had forced a rather relaxed academic schedule. Nigel had just enough time to give his hair a quick comb before racing to class.

'Oh well, looks aren't everything,' his mirror said tartly.

'Get cracked!' Nigel yelled as he left the room.

Chapter Six

QUESTIONABLE AUTHORITY

'I can't see why the Reunion was cancelled,' Barry said, as he and Ermine walked from Dorco's spiffy new grave in the Malfeasance family plot. It was in a dank little corner of a Dork cemetery next to the Stalins. 'I mean, these things happen.'

'Barry, the man died,' Ermine said.

'About bloody time,' Barry said. 'I should've killed him back at school. J.G. always convinced me not to. "I need him for the story," she said. Like anybody ever read *his* bits.'

'I resent that!' the ghost Dorco said, wafting by.

'Sorry,' Ermine said. 'You looked very natural.' But Dorco had gone, off to do whatever it is ghosts do all day.

'Look at this epitaph,' Barry said, pointing at a headstone. '"It Could Be Worse."'

Chuckling, Barry and Ermine evaporated, and drifted back to Hogwash. As they sat on a bench outside in the sun, waiting for the dampness to leave their clothes, Ermine looked pensive.

'What are you thinking about?' Barry said, putting his hand on top of Ermine's tenderly.

'How Dorco gave me crabs.' Barry removed his hand. He wasn't sure if she was joking or not. Just in case, he tried to move away from her using his buttock muscles alone.

'So. Any idea who might've broken that *Ann-Margaret* spell?' she said. Grand entrance spells such as that one were powerful magic, seldom seen outside a Hogsbleede dinner theatre.

Barry was using his wand to direct two armies of ants against each other. What to him was sport was to these ants the Battle of the Early Afternoon, the defining moment of their civilisation.

'Barry?'

'What? Get 'im!'

'It's not nice to enchant things smaller than you. Answer my question: do you know who broke Dorco's spell?'

'No, but if you figure it out, let me know their address, I'd like to send them one hell of a fruit basket.'

'I'm serious, Barry,' Ermine said.

'So am I!'

'It's murder, you know. He didn't just fall; for a man that big, Dorco wasn't clumsy. No, somebody *killed* the Headmister,' Ermine said. 'And we have to find out who.'

'Why, to send them a thank-you note?' Barry said. 'It's a gift horse, Erm – why must you count *every* filling?'

'I can't help it,' Ermine said with a smile. 'Dentists' daughter, you know.'

''Scuse us,' Barry said, jockeying past a Muddle couple. The steps of Hogwash were a popular place for Muddles to propose (and occasionally consummate) marriage. When they walked into the building, Barry and Ermine were met by Ludicrous Malfeasance. His countenance was more sour than usual.

'We're very sorry for your loss,' Ermine said.

'What loss? He's already moved in with Neurotica and I,' Ludicrous said bitterly. 'I keep saying, "Being a ghost means you can STOP EATING!"' he groused. 'Sitting around watching television, making the sofa all cold . . . He could never do anything right, that kid, not even die. Most people croak and leave you in peace,' Ludicrous said. 'Not *that* poltergit.'

'Oh,' Ermine said, unsure of herself. This was a grey area, as far as her etiquette books were concerned.

'Hullo folks,' Hafwid said. He was leading Professor Mumblemumble through the entry hall. 'Givin' a turr.'

'A truly amazing building,' Mumblemumble said. 'You don't see water damage like this any more.'

Hafwid smiled; after working for so long at the school, he took all compliments to it personally. 'U'm gonna miss this plac',' he said.

'Miss it? Where are you going?' Barry asked. Who the hell would employ Hafwid? Couldn't they smell his breath?

'Oh, it ain't jus' me,' Hafwid said, waving his arms (and in doing so, dispersing giant armpit reekings far and wide). 'We're all goin'. T'Atlantis.'

'Idiot!' Mumblemumble screeched. A big vaporous fist shot out of his wand and hammered Hafwid on the top of the head, driving him like a giant, pickled nail.

Barry, Ermine and Malfeasance stared; nobody treated Hafwid like that, not if they wanted to keep all their internal organs present and accounted for. Barry had seen Bumblemore smack Hafwid once or twice, but Bumblemore wasn't around any more. And maybe that was why.

The foreign professor noticed their reaction and said, 'I am sorry, my custom may seem strange. This is how we show our enthusiasm.' The fist came down again. 'I am very interested in what Mr Hafwid is saying.'

In between winces, Hafwid laughed nervously. 'I meen, whut I sed was, ha ha, we're not tryin' to sell Hogwash' – the vapour-fist smacked him again – ''cuz we won' need it'– smack! – 'after the spell gets casted' – smack! – 'an' we're all gone.'

Hafwid sidestepped the final swat, and asked, 'Whut're yeh hittin me fer? I didn't tell thum whoo yeh rilly are.'

'Arrghh!' Mumblemumble gave a bellow of rage. 'Fool!' He grabbed the giant's callusy mitt, pulling uselessly. 'Come on,' he said, then gave up and stalked off.

'Sorry, Barry, I've already tol' yoo too much,' Hafwid said. 'I s'pose.' Shrugging his shoulders, he lumbered off towards his new, abusive pal.

'What was that about?' Ermine said. 'Am I the only one who doesn't understand a word Hafwid says? Might the school spring for a speech therapist or something?'

Ludicrous whispered – the odd pair were only twenty feet away. 'This new Professor Mumblemumble comes with excellent made-up credentials, but don't know if I quite trust him.'

'Well, he's just Dork Arts and Crafts prof,' Ermine said. 'Wait a bit and he'll die or something.'

'True, true. Anyway . . .' Ludicrous took several quick, deep breaths as if to steady himself, then said in a firm, loud voice – speaking as if to convince himself it was really happening – 'Barry, the Trustees would like you to be Interim Headmister of Hogwash. Do you accept?' Ludicrous looked as though each word had been dipped in ipecac.

'SWEET CHRIST!' they heard Mumblemumble exclaim.

'Is there a problem over there?' Ludicrous called out, looking over Barry's shoulder.

'No, no probl'm,' Hafwid said, over a stream of choked nonsense coming out of the professor's mouth. 'Jus' more enthusiasum.' The giant was shoving Mumblemumble outside with some difficulty.

'Let me at him!' Mumblemumble hollered. He seemed to be frothing. 'Just one quick spell! I'll fix his wagon!'

'Git ahold of yerself, Prof'ss'r – rememb'r our mishun,' Hafwid said, and the door closed. Barry, Ermine and Ludicrous could still hear swearing and several thumps, as Mumblemumble apparently threw himself against the door.

Ludricrous made the 'crazy' gesture at his temple,

then the trio turned back to the discussion at hand. 'Anyway . . .' Ludicrous said.

'You want me to be Headmister?' Barry was truly surprised to be asked, and Ermine was truly annoyed not to be. 'Why me, Ludicrous? You hate me.'

'Yes, Barry. Yes, I do.' He was a little too comfortable admitting this for Barry's taste.

'So do I have to teach a class?' Barry said.

'Our insurance company, Eternal Life, is insisting that you don't,' Ludicrous said. 'They think you're a lawsuit waiting to happen, especially with all these Americans walking around.'[25]

[25] Always looking to make a quick Gallon, several Dork Trustees had used several pounds of raw steak to convince then-Headmister Lon Measly to let in wealthy foreign students. Within a term of the programme's founding, a group of Americans had threatened a class-action lawsuit, claiming that the torches and braziers used around the school 'produced dangerous levels of secondhand smoke'.

The affable Lon was totally unsuited to fighting off this attack. So the Trustees found a pretext to remove him – he was discovered *in flagrante* with a Pomeranian, and even though three is well past the age of consent for a dog, 'Hogwash Headmister Nabbed in Tryst With Three-Year-Old' is the kind of headline that freezes the blood. In exchange for keeping it quiet, Lon stepped down without a fight.

Ludicrous was charged with finding a suitable replacement. It took him approximately fifteen seconds to decide upon his son, Dorco. It took slightly longer to arrange the bribes, but 'where there

Barry was puzzled. 'So, you hate me, and I can't teach the students—'

'Even informally. They wanted me to make you wear a gag, but I said you might suffocate.'

'Then by Mrs Merlin's merkin, why are you asking me to be Headmister?' Barry exclaimed. 'Why not Erm, here? She's a suck-up.' (She secretly pinched him.)

'Barry, this is a very delicate time – first the theme park, now Dorco's death – and keeping good relations with the Muddle world is essential,' Ludicrous said. 'Headmister of Hogwash is a high-profile spot, and the Trustees feel that you would make an excellent figurehead. We want Ermine to actually make all the decisions, of course. She will be Interim Headmistress.'

Her ego salved, Ermine asked the length of the term. Still, Barry could tell something was bothering his wife.

'As long as it takes to find a suitable candidate,' Ludicrous said. 'Could be two weeks, could be two years. Whatever happens, we can't have the Muddles

are Gallons flowing, fair winds are blowing,' and the deal got done. In return, the non-Dork Trustees were allowed to fill a tenured position, and they picked Author Measly just to piss Ludicrous off.

Dorco's first act as Headmister set the tone for the ruthless reign to come: he settled with the students out of court; then he made them kill themselves – after first willing the money to him personally. This is how one can build an immense pleasure barge on a teacher's salary.

stop coming. That's what's paying for the theme park we're building out in the lake.' Hogwash: The Experience was Ludicrous's big score, but this joint venture between the Trustees and Lord Valumart was already way over budget, as well as six months behind schedule thanks to labour problems with the dwarves. Another delay could doom the project. If this happened, not only would the Malfeasance family fortune disappear, Lord Valumart would surely dispatch some hit-wizards after him. 'So, do you accept?' Ludicrous asked.

Barry looked at Ermine, who was mouthing the word 'no' silently, over and over.

'We'll do it,' he said.

'Excellent,' Ludicrous said, then spied Author Measly, his arms full of books, over Ermine's shoulder. 'If you'll excuse me—' The old Dork nutjob sprinted away. Measly saw him just in time, dropped his books and ran, robes fluttering behind him. Malfeasance took a wild swipe with his silverfish-headed walking stick, and the pair turned a corner out of sight.

Now they were alone, Barry asked Ermine, 'What's your problem? You're Headmistress too. If you're worried about Fiona, she can stay with your parents until we get settled,' Barry said. 'Then she can come and live with us here.'

'This is the last place I want her,' Ermine said. 'I think you might have just signed our death warrants.'

'Why?' Barry asked.

'The old Headmister has died – you didn't kill him, did you?' Ermine asked. 'That would be utterly like you.'

'No,' Barry said.

'Then someone has killed the Headmister, and now we might be next.'

'Oh, you're such a worrywart,' Barry said. 'Think of the prestige, the respect, the big parking space . . .'

'Big enough for a Dragonette Decimator, I'd imagine,' Ermine said, angling as always. What she wanted was never far from her thoughts.

Immediately, Barry sent a cell-owl[26] to Ferd and Jorge, inviting them to come and celebrate. Ferd and Jorge responded immediately, and condensed inside the Grittyfloor Guest Quarters about an hour later.

'Sorry we couldn't change into formal robes,' Ferd said.

'Yeah, there wasn't time,' Jorge said. He was looking at the book produced specially for the Reunion. Colin

[26] Cell-owls worked like normal owls, except they were the size of a single cell. Much more portable, they were also easier to lose.

had dug up some old photos, which made it rather gripping. Jorge turned it lengthwise. 'I didn't even realise we *had* a Mud-Wrestling Team.'

'Formal robes, coming up,' Ermine said, changing the subject. She conjured two sets of formal robes with a snap. Not coincidentally, two octogenarians in the process of receiving honorary degrees from Cambridge became stark naked.

'Uh, Ermine,' Barry said, remembering his tour with Nigel, 'let's keep the conjuring to a minimum, okay?'

'Why?' his wife said.

'It puts cellulite on the hips,' Barry said, smacking a haunch. The truth was too long a story for the moment, and to Ermine that was a threat with real teeth. He turned to the twins. 'Well chaps, can I mix you a potion?'

Since the death of their previous Headmister, the students had been running wild, so much so that the house elves wouldn't perform basic tasks for fear of being abducted and eaten. So the first thing Ermine did that evening at dinner was cast an ancient spell. '*Warning,*' she intoned, '*due to the graphic nature of what you are about to see, parental discretion is advised.*' The entire room went silent, looking at the High Table with complete attention.

'It's a hormonal thing,' she explained. 'But talk quickly, before they realise there's no nudity.'

Head Trustee Malfeasance stood up, revealing his golden truss, the symbol of his office. 'Students, following the death of my son Dorco' – the spectre, sitting at the Ghosts' Table, waved clasped fists like a boxer – 'the Trustees of Hogwash have decided that the interim Headmister and Headmistress will be Barry Trotter and Ermine Cringer.'

There was no real reaction to the news, except that Severe Snipe began walking down the length of the Silverfish table, distributing cups of his homemade Death Draught to anybody who asked.[27] (He was too close to his pension to do away with himself.)

After Ludicrous sat down, Barry got up to say something, but the complete silence and sea of blank expressions discouraged him. Only Nigel had a big smile on his face, and was giving an enthusiastic thumbs-up. With his parents running the school, the balance of power swung away from the bullies and towards Nigel and Junior rather decisively.

[27] In town for the Reunion, Flabbe and Oyle had killed themselves immediately after Dorco's death, rather than face the wrath of all the people they had bullied. After death, they found work in advertisements for F.X. Potts's Multi-Flavour Sleeping Pills.

'Uh, thanks a lot,' Barry said. 'My wife and I will try to do our best.' He sat down.

'Our door is always open,' Ermine added.

'Did you say "Dork"?' shouted a voice from the Silverfish table.

'DOOR, as in come and visit if you're ever thinking of doing away with yourself,' Ermine said. 'Dead students don't become giving alumni.'

'Being dead is great!' Dorco chimed in.

'Shh!' Nurse Pommefritte scolded.

'I mean, awful,' Dorco said, wearing an exaggerated frown. 'Also, stay away from drugs.'

'An' booz',' Hafwid said, then passed out cold. Some house elves scurried out with a stretcher.

'Oh, leave him,' Barry said, making his first decision as Headmister. 'Let's eat.'

Barry found that he enjoyed his new prestige. He found that the power of life and death over all Hogwash students, faculty, alumni and friends made being called 'Most Likely to Become a Lay Gynaecologist' in the spoof Reunion book easier to take. Barry felt so good, so magnanimous, that he realised he must've been quite an unrelenting arsewipe as a kid to annoy Bumblemore as much as he remembered having done.

Barry felt a sudden, unfamiliar rush of gratitude. He

raised his glass. 'To Alpo Bumblemore, that rackety old pillow-biter, wherever he is!'

'Hear, hear!'

Mumblemumble stood up and said, 'You are too kind.'

'What?' Ermine said.

Realising his error, the new professor hastily stumbled towards an excuse. 'Uh – I'm just practising dialogue from my new play.'

'What's it called?' Barry asked.

Mumblemumble cast about wildly. 'Uh . . . "A Moment of . . . Confused Discomfort"?'

Ferd made a face. 'I wouldn't go and see anything called that.'

'I've done a little writing,' Barry said, 'and I can tell you: that stinks.'

'It's only a working title,' Mumblemumble said. 'Do you have any suggestions?'

'Yeah,' Jorge said, his mouth full of food. 'How about "Shaggin"?'

'Sounds too much like a musical,' Ferd said. 'How about "An Evening of Supermodels in the Altogether"?'

'Smashing,' Jorge said, and the topic changed.

As Barry and Ermine ate, they discussed what had happened – to Dorco, and the rest of it. Lon was under the table, begging for scraps. Barry gave him a fatty bit of prime rib.

'Thanks,' Lon said.

'So, Mr Former Headmister, do you have any advice for me?' Barry asked.

'Don't lick yourself after dinner,' Lon said. 'Also, don't try to sniff the Trustees' arses. They get weird about it.'

'That's never been one of my enthusiasms,' Barry said.

'You have no idea what you're missing.'

Barry preferred not to think about it. 'How is it working out with Hafwid?'

'Oh, fine,' Lon said. 'I miss Genny. Hafwid and this new Dork Arts and Crafts professor are up to something. I heard 'em talking last night in Hafwid's hut.'

'Really? What did they say?'

'I think I might need another piece of prime rib to remember,' Lon said. Barry gave him one.

'I can't remember,' Lon said.

'Hey, that's not fair!' Barry said indignantly. 'If I give you another piece of meat, you're supposed to tell me what you know!'

'I don't know very much,' Lon said. 'Not much space,' he said, tapping his temple, then getting his finger stuck in the hole there.

Disgusted, Barry rejoined the table. Halfway through the second course, Ermine whispered, 'Barry, I think that man is Alpo Bumblemore.'

'Who, him? That guy three chairs down?' Barry said, mouth full, jabbing the air with his knife. The new professor was shaking his head, while mouthing the word 'no' and waving his hands.

'Way to be secret-y!' Ermine said. 'Yes, him.'

'You mean the guy with the long, white facial hair—'

'Coincidence,' Mumblemumble said.

'– the identity-obscuring balaclava—'

'Psoriasis,' Mumblemumble said.

'– wearing Alpo's old hat—'

'It's cold and flu season,' the man said. 'Draughty!'

'– is Headmister Bumblemore?' Barry asked.

'Yes.'

'That's insane. Everybody knows Bumblemore is dead. All those morning-after potions you took at school must've scrambled your brains.' Ermine *had* taken a lot of them. Nurse Pommefritte even called them 'Cringers', though Ermine said that it was because after you took one once, you'd instinctively curl up to protect your innards whenever you thought of it.

'Whoa!' Ferd said. 'Harshing on Ermine!'

'You didn't used to let him get away with stuff like that,' said Jorge.

'Yes, you idiot,' Ermine said, ignoring the twins' banter. 'And what's more, I think he was responsible for Dorco's death.'

'I totally wasn't,' Mumblemumble said earnestly.

Ermine gave him a dirty look. 'Mind your own business!' Then to Barry: 'Maybe we should have this conversation somewhere more private, away from the rabble.'

'Give some people power and they get all high and mighty,' the professor said. 'When I was Headmister—'

'HA!' Ermine said.

'– sorry, slip of the tongue – *if I ever were* Headmister, I'd be more democratic and, frankly, nicer to somebody I wasn't paying very much, unless I'd like to be the one teaching how to make death curses out of paper plates, macaroni and glue.'

'Dork Arts and Crafts is cinchy,' Ermine said.

'Yeah?' the professor said. 'Tell me how to make a God's-eye.'

'Well, first you take some multicoloured yarn—'

'WRONG! The lolly sticks come first.'

'People, people, stop acting like children,' Barry said, 'That's my job. Anyway, I don't think Professor Mumblemumble here broke Dorco's *Ann-Margaret* spell. That's absurd.'

Ermine leaned back and took a sip from her flagon. 'And who do you think it was?'

Barry took another bite of were-steak. 'I think it was Snipe.'

Everyone at the table let out various noises of disagreement. Below, Lon bumped his head on the table in surprise. Snipe himself was circulating among the several suicidal Silverfishers, taking down their final anti-Trotter imprecations and generally making their last minutes on Earth as comfortable as possible.

'Do you have any evidence for this theory?' Ferd asked.

'None whatsoever,' Barry said. 'But we always suspected Snipe back in the old days and well, I'm a traditionalist.'

'Or a moron . . .' Ermine muttered.

'Did you say something, darling?' Barry asked.

'Nothing, dear,' Ermine said sweetly.

'That Herbology professor of ours can pack it away,' Barry said. 'Just Doritos and biscuits, eh Madame Sprig?' She nodded, smiling dreamily, with pupils the size of dinner plates.

Barry turned to the foreign professor. 'Where's "Mumblemumble" from, anyway? What nationality is it?'

The odd man coughed nervously, saying something like, 'Tingo-Jingo.'

'I've never heard of it,' Ermine said.

'Well, you wouldn't have,' Mumblemumble said. 'It's very exclusive.'

'What's the deal with the balaclava?' Ferd asked.

'Tingo-Jingo is much warmer than here. I'm still getting used to the climate.' The man mock-shivered to make everybody laugh. When nobody did, they broke the uncomfortable moment by moving on to other topics.

'Must do something about that Grittyfloor Quiddit team,' Ferd said.

Ermine jumped in. 'Hey, I thought the mask was for psoriasis,' she said.

Barry raised his voice. 'For God's sake, woman, will you stop hounding the man?'

'Don't you yell at me!' Ermine said.

'I'm Headmister! I'll yell at whoever I want!'

'So am I! So there!' Ermine responded.

Jorge stepped in. 'Barry, Ermine, don't fight in front of the children. Do it later, when you can use profanity.'

Barry looked out at the sea of squabbling students, all happily wasting food, taunting each other and hatching innumerable plots that would harness their youthful vigour and ingenuity in the most useless and destructive ways.

'Look at them,' Barry said.

'What, the desserts?' Ferd said.

Barry performed a quick auto-biffing spell, and an unseen force slapped Ferd on the back of the head. 'No, the students,' he said. Barry felt a surge of pride. '*My* students.'

Ermine kicked him under the table.

'Hey! Why do you always resort to violence?' Barry asked, rubbing his shin.

'Why do you always resort to stupidity?' Ermine said. Barry frowned, then returned to what he had been saying.

'The future of wizarding – it's all in their hands,' Barry said, regaining his expansiveness.

'I'm suddenly seized with an urge to apply for Muddleship,' Jorge said.

'What I wouldn't give to be young again!' Barry mused. 'Remember what it was like?'

'Only vaguely,' Madame Sprig admitted.

'I think I speak for the entire faculty when I say, "Thank God it's over,"' Snipe said. He had returned, his duties as Angel of Death complete.

'You'd wake up full of energy—' Barry said.

'– with a fresh pimple right between your eyes,' Ferd said.

'Full of plans and dreams –' Barry said.

'– none of which you could do anything about, because no adult would let you,' Jorge said.

'Maybe you had a crush on somebody –' Barry said.

'– or everybody,' Ferd said, looking at Ermine, who transferred her kicking to him. 'Ow!'

'Some beautiful girl –' Barry said.

'– who didn't even know you existed,' Snipe said. Snipe liked girls? Who knew? Barry threw his napkin down on the table in annoyance (it promptly folded itself). 'Oh, you're just jealous,' he said. 'Jealous that you're not young like they are.'

'No, Barry, we remember what being a teenager was really like,' Ermine said. 'We've had less wine than you have.'

'I think you're wrong,' Barry said. 'I'm going to go down there and find out what they think.'

'I wouldn't recommend it,' said Snipe, who was polishing off some of Hogwash's famously dry pot roast. Apparently his grisly duties with the Silverfishers – a full third of whom had willingly poisoned themselves and been removed by house elves wearing little biohazard suits – hadn't affected his appetite.

'Barry Trotter, Man of the People,' Ermine said facetiously.

Barry was annoyed. 'Erm, I don't see how it could hurt. I mean, you're behind the scenes and I'm out front. Happy students is part of my job.'

'Suit yourself,' Ermine said.

'Do you mind if I come?' Mumblemumble said. 'I would like to see this.'

'Certainly,' Barry said. 'You will see what a fine type of wizard and witch we are producing at Hogwash.' The pair carried their plates down the riser and over to the Pufnstuf Table.

'Do you mind if we sit and "rap" with you?' Barry said. The students grumbled their assent, moving over to make room.

'You're totally not Barry Trotter,' a big kid with a red cowlick said as they sat down.

'I totally am,' Barry said. 'I'm curious, why do you say that?'

'I read all the books,' the kid said. 'You're too short. Plus, Barry's much cooler.'

'I promise you, I am.' Barry was momentarily stymied, then reached into his robes and pulled out his wallet. He took out his Evaporating Licence. 'Lousy picture.' He handed it to the kid. 'If it's not me, I feel sorry for whoever it is.' He turned to the foreign professor to share a 'isn't it horrible being old?' moment. The professor smiled weakly.

The kid, unimpressed, handed it back. 'You can get a better fake for five bleedin' Gnutts in Hogsbleede.'

'Look, you can see my forehead, right?'

'From space.' The kids snickered. 'Where's that famous "unruly mop of hair", eh?'

Barry really didn't like this kid. 'In my hairbrushes, thanks for reminding me.'

Barry was losing control; dissent spread. 'Make a big pile of Gallons appear,' a spotty girl demanded.

'An' give 'em to me,' another boy added rudely, with an outsized guffaw.

Barry started to incant, but remembered poor Henratty. 'I can't . . .'

'Told ya,' the cowlicked boy said, folding his arms.

'I mean, I *can* – it's elementary–'

'Sure.'

'– but I won't, and anyway ten points from whatever your House is, for cheek.'

'Go ahead, it's Grittyfloor,' the boy said. 'We never win anyway.'

Barry was outraged. 'But why are you sitting over here at the Pufnstuf table?'

'These are my friends. Anyway, it's a free country.'

'No, it's not!' Barry spluttered for lack of anything

better to say. Insolent *and* lacking in House spirit! He was appalled. Surely he hadn't been as obnoxious as this young creep. 'Look, you may think you're funny, but really you're just embarrassing yourself and the school in front of this visiting professor from Tingo-Jingo.'

The kid burst out laughing at the name. The others joined in.

'Oh, you may think your pals are laughing with you, but you know what they're really thinking? They're really thinking, Wow [your name] is a real jerk. I think it's really "rad" – or perhaps "def" or "phat" – that Headmister Trotter came down to hang out with us and get the "four one one" on "my magi-peeps and myself".'

The laughter continued. Then it dawned on Barry; a slight smile broke across his face. He knew this kid's game. 'You're testing me because I'm new Headmister. You wouldn't do this to Dorco. Or Alpo Bumblemore.'

'Who's he?' the kid said insolently. Mumblemumble's arm whipped into the air as if to strike the student, but he stopped himself and pretended to adjust his pointy hat.

'Oh, right, you mean that wee wand from the books.'

'Gah!' The foreign professor emitted a strangled cry and sprang at the student. Barry had to physically restrain him, though the student obviously felt no fear.

'I think you'd better leave, young man,' Barry

squeezed out amid the effort of restraining the foreign professor. 'What's your name, so I can dock your House properly?'

'Barry Trotter,' the kid said with a smirk as he and his mates got up. They'd left a huge mess for the house elves.

'Very funny! I'll find out who you are, and when I do,' Barry shouted, 'it'll be a HUNDRED points from Grittyfloor!' The kids walked out, utterly unconcerned. Barry relaxed his grip and released Mumblemumble. Panting, he went back to the High Table.

'How'd it go, man of the people?' Ermine said, smirking, when Barry returned to his seat.

'Don't smirk,' Barry said angrily. 'Dorco used to smirk, and look what happened to him!' The Great Hall suddenly hushed: had Barry finally settled his score with Dorco? God knew, but He wasn't telling. Good, let that rumour spread, Barry thought. Maybe if they think I'm a killer, these myrrh-huffing little bastards will show a little respect.

Chapter Seven

SIR GODAWFLE'S GROTTO

The next day, Nigel and Junior sat passing notes in Notions. In previous years, this infraction had been serious – the first person caught each term was beheaded, and his/her noggin put on a spike at the front of the class as a warning (and ten points was taken from Grittyfloor). But no longer. Snipe didn't seem to care.

'The thimble is perhaps the most powerful of all magical sewing aids,' the sallow professor read listlessly from tear-stained lecture notes. 'Never underestimate its power.'

'Do you like Yvonne Bognor? Tick yes or no,' the note read. Nigel ticked 'no'. Feeling bad, he added 'but she seems nice', then passed it back. Over the course of an hour, he had given opinions on most of the school, mostly truthful. He had lied on the 'Are You a Prude?' quiz – he hadn't really 'gone under the bra' yet.

It was harmless, typical nonsense, but such nonsense made even less sense at Hogwash, given the easy availability of love charms, potions and philtres. Affections shifted by the day, or hour. Within days of arriving at school, every single student was under the influence of some magical something or other – and if one factored in that the hexing student was probably hexed him/herself, by someone who themselves was being magically manipulated – well, it was fantastically complex. Normally, the vigilance of teachers like Snipe kept the fires of love (and hate) damped down somewhat, but today Snipe's heart wasn't in it. Or in much else for that matter. The blackboard was usually crammed with complex diagrams, but all that was written on it today was 'I am NOT Headmister'.

The bell rang, and there was a flurry of book-closing. 'Curse-crossstitch takes a lot of practice, so remember to do your homework. Or don't do it, it doesn't matter.'

The entire class double-taked as one.

'You heard me,' Snipe said dejectedly. 'It doesn't matter. Apparently you can flunk out for years, and still become Headmister.' The once-feared Professor of Notions collapsed into sobs. The class filed out with embarrassment, which turned to laughter and cruel impressions as soon as they reached the corridor.

Snipe's class was the end of the day, and Nigel and

Junior were hungry. They did something that every first-year does once, and only once: bought a chocolate bar from the vending machines outside the gents' on the second floor.

Junior tore it in half so they could share. As he did so, a bloodcurdling scream was heard.

'I knew it was stale,' Nigel said, 'but it didn't look undead.'

'Whatever it is, yuck,' Junior said. 'Let's go to Godawfle's.'

'Yeah,' Nigel said. 'The food there may be terrible, but at least it won't complain.'

So off they tromped to the Grittyfloor Buttery. Every House had one – these student lounges were one of the finest innovations of the late, not-so-great Malfeasance Administration. Silverfish's was the best, of course – it was Dorco's pleasure barge, refitted, magically shielded from the weather, bobbing decadently out on the lake.

It took them for ever – the stairs kept rearranging themselves; what a pain in the backside *that* always was – but eventually they arrived at 'Sir Godawfle's Grotto', half in honour of the founder of the House, and half in the mistaken belief that giving a place a funny name makes the diners resent lousy food less. At Hogwash, as at most schools, the majority of calories consumed were of the cheap junk-food variety, pizzas conjured quick and popped in the microwave, burgers wolfed down on the way to Professor Bunns's class.[28]

The Grotto was cosy and convivial, with a big-screen scrying ball showing international Quiddit (or one of the endless re-runs of 'What Not to Were', depending on who got to the set first). There were a few pinball machines, current magazines, couches to stretch out on and no surly house elves – it was really one of the homiest places in the entire school. They even let you bring in your familiar. Junior now wanted an octopus, like Chesterfield. (His goat had been abducted for immoral purposes by the centaurs.) The boys had formed a secret club called 'Friends of the Octopi', or FOTO.[29]

[28] You didn't actually think that the students took all their meals in the Great Hall, did you? Do you have any idea how much that would *cost*? One can't blame J.G. Rollins for only describing the spooky and impressive elements of Hogwash. She knew what would sell. A janitor's closet is the same whether you're attending Hogwash or Hubert Humphrey High, so J.G. played up the vaulted ceilings and grand staircases and huge barking paintings of dogs playing poker, and left the crumbling cornices, raging mouse problem, and ancient thirty-gallon drums of Spew-B-Gon in the earlier, unedited drafts.

[29] FOTO's rules were:

1) Each member must have an octopus, or *really* want one.
2) Each member must kiss an octopus on the beak at least once.
3) Each member must do the Octopus Dance in public once a

'Have you ever seen the Radishgnaw Buttery?' Junior said. 'I heard there's a familiar fighting ring.'

'Wow,' Nigel said, not knowing whether he was supposed to think that was cool or awful. So he changed the subject. 'Do you want a Rhutastic?'

At the same time as they subcontracted out the Picking Cap, Hogwash had hired out the operations of each of the House Butteries to appropriate hotel catering firms. By appropriate, I mean that Silverfish's cuisine was decidedly more evil, prepared by a megalomaniacal firm.[30] The food for Grittyfloor was provided by an EU branch of Taste Sensations.

The only thing wrong with the Grotto was that it was absolutely infested with mice. Since the site was the basilisp's old lair deep underground, it had withstood the lethal special effects of Wagner Bros and had become the natural refuge for Hogwash's rebellious

day, with certain customised personal moves that CANNOT BE STOLEN by another member.

4) No member can reveal the secrets of the club to any 'common fish' (non-members) on pain of death by strangulation. This will be done by smearing boiled shrimps on your neck and letting Chesterfield grab it.

The only FOTO secret so far was that Junior liked a Pufnstuf named Lauren.

[30] You WILL Eat This, plc, a wholly owned subsidiary of Valumart Enterprises.

rodents, who were led by an unkillable mouse named Timothy.[31]

Most days, Hogwash's mice were busy foraging, or fending off the Burrowers, who hunted them for meat. But as luck would have it, today was Timothy's birthday and he was celebrating it by bungee jumping from the chandeliers. At a table twelve feet below, three Grittyfloor sixth-years were having a heart-to-heart-to-heart.

'Evelyn, has Aidan ever asked you to, erm, clear-cut the forbidden forest?' a girl called Elizabeth asked.

'The forbidden what?' Evelyn said.

Elizabeth pointed down to her lap.

'Oh no! I wouldn't. I'd be afraid of ingrown hairs,' Evelyn said. 'I bet Jane has.' They all laughed as attention was turned to Jane.

'I went crazy with a razor once,' Jane said. 'I was shaving my legs and just kept going. It itched like mad while it was growing back.'

'And why the sudden interest in the topiary arts?' Evelyn asked archly.

'Well –' Elizabeth took a gulp of fizzy drink and

[31] Details of how this mouse became immortal can be found in *Barry Trotter and the Shameless Parody*. (No, I'm not going to tell you. Buy the damn book!)

spoke through some ice-cubes. 'Ian has asked me to, but I'm not sure.'

'Make him do it too!' Jane said; they all laughed in encouragement.

High above, Timothy was strapping in. 'Guys, I may not be drunk enough to do this,' he said. 'You think that last jump by Big Cheese stretched the rope out?'

'Don't be a wuss!' Timothy's friend Dexter chided.

'I mean, I can't die,' Timothy said. 'It's just that—'

Before Timothy could even finish his sentence, Dexter pushed him off the chandelier. All Timothy's friends, most of them three mouse-sized sheets to the wind (thanks to a puddle of beer underneath one of the tables), cheered lustily and profanely.

The girls below continued chatting, unaware that for them, Life was about to get a lot grosser.

'I've got a "Morgana le Fay",' Elizabeth said.

'A what?' Evelyn asked.

'You shave one side, and wear a "comb-over",' Elizabeth said.

Timothy was right – Big Cheese had stretched the rope; he landed on the table with a disgustingly crunchy sound, then was yanked back up. He left a bloody little silhouette on the tablecloth.

'Look, a mouse fell on our table,' Jane said.

'Oh well, it's gone now,' Elizabeth said, not realising Tim was merely on the rebound.

'That's disgusting,' Evelyn said. 'Cover it up with something.'

Elizabeth moved her mug of hot tea. Timothy came back down, and was dunked.

'Ahh!' he squeaked, quick-poached. 'This sucks!'

'Gross!' Elizabeth said. 'That mouse got blood in my tea.'

'I'll give you a Gallon if you drink it,' Evelyn said.

'I think some's in my hair, too,' Elizabeth said, feeling her head.

'Look!' said Jane, pointing at the chandelier. 'there's loads more "blood mice"!' (She had just coined the term.)

'Disgusting,' Elizabeth said. 'Let's go and watch *Changing Dooms*.'[32]

'No, I've got to start doing my homework,' Jane said. 'Somebody should tell Fistuletta.'

The girls left. Fistuletta was one of the lunch ladies, a giantess. She was 347, covered with warts, piles, skin-tags, and tufts of hair jutting out of unsettling places, which made her quite a bombshell. Though she was

[32] This show, one of ValuVision's biggest hits, allowed neighbours to exchange the circumstances of their deaths. The only shows more popular than this involved using magic to make fools of Muddles.

unmarried, Fistuletta was holding out for somebody better than Hafwid.

Timothy was coming in and out of a coma as he bounced up and down above the table; his friends were cheering wildly and waiting for the bouncing to subside, so they could haul him up. On his last trip down, Timothy revived just enough to notice that the table of girls had left.

'That's right . . .' he said weakly. 'You . . . better run.'

Then poor Timothy descended a little more, and saw Fistuletta.

'Oh no . . .' he said.

She grabbed the mouse and crushed it in her fist. High above, a small, squeaky cheer went up. Getting Timothy killed – then watching him come back to life – was simply great entertainment. It never got old (to them at least).

'Clean-up at table three! It's a wet one!' Fistuletta bellowed, and a house elf with a bucket and a mop trudged out of the kitchen, grumbling to himself.

Chapter Eight

EXTREME QUIDDIT

When Barry arrived at his and Ermine's new digs – the Headmister's Office! – bright and early on Monday morning, there was already a line of students outside. Madame Ponce stood behind them, tapping her mary-jane shod foot. Ponce, the school's Librarian, was an excessively bony, scrawny woman who Barry suspected was really a man.

'Good morning, girls. Good morning, Madame Ponce. How is the Library?' Barry said. 'Did any books escape in the night?' (This was a constant problem.)

'The library would be *fine*, if some students would remember that it is a place of scholarship, and not' – her expression dipped down deep into disgust – 'a strip club.'

'Strip club, eh?' Barry's interest level suddenly exploded. 'Come in and tell me about it,' he said, ushering the group in.

'We were in the Reserved Section!' one girl said. She was upset. 'It wasn't like we wanted people to see.'

'Are you going to tell our parents?' said another, near tears.

'Madame Ponce, tell me the details of this outrage,' Barry said, fighting a smile.

'I don't see what's so funny,' she said. 'Alpo Bumblemore wouldn't've—'

'I'm not Alpo,' Barry said, with the slightest hint of an edge. Ermine walked in with a bottomless cup of coffee.[33]

'Well, I found these – hussies – swabbing swelling solution on their, their—'

'Chests?' Ermine chirped. She handed one of the girls a tissue to blow her nose.

'Yes,' Madame Ponce said with repugnance.

'Oh, we all try it once, don't we?' Ermine said good-naturedly.

'*No,*' Madame Ponce said.

Misery loves company – apparently so does flat-chestedness, Barry thought. From his office window he could see several students aloft over the Quiddit pitch,

[33] This elementary wizard spell drove the Muddle firm Starbucks out of business.

and by the wobbliness of their flight Barry bet they were from Grittyfloor. He turned to his wife. 'This seems like a job for the Head*mistress*,' he said. 'Do you mind handling it?'

'No, but we—'

'Great. I've got some paperwork to do.'

At the desk across the room, Barry began writing out a personal ad in Snipe's name. 'It's Not the Meat, It's the Notions,' Barry wrote. 'Respected academic, sallow, 6'0", 165, short of temper, wand, looking for open-minded companion/familiar. I enjoy puppies, long walks on the beach, fisting. Let's take points from Grittyfloor together. No fatties.' Now to post it to the *Daily Soothsayer*; he put on his 'Hunting With Hafwid' windbreaker and strolled over to where Ermine was overseeing the girls' detention. (After writing out a spell for them to slip inside their training bras.)

'I'm just going to pop over to the owleteria, then to the Quiddit field,' he said, already at the door. 'Probably won't be back before lunch.'

'But Barry, we have to—'

'I know,' Barry said, with no idea. 'And we will. Later.' He'd figure out how to dodge it again, whatever it was, when the time came. 'Tootle-oo, girls. Remember, more than a champagne flute's worth is overkill.' Barry left the room, whistling. Nicely done, he thought.

'Ms Cringer, may I be a lesbian?' one girl asked, watching Barry leave the room.

'I know how you feel,' Ermine replied in a sisterly way. 'Imagine being married to it.'

First, a quick trip into the smelly, mite-infested owleteria. Barry was wise enough not to ask Earwig to take his note. After her throat surgery he insisted she quit smoking, and with a flurry of innumerable nips and slashes ever since, she had told him that his correspondence was no longer welcome in her feet. Her wind was terrible anyway – she couldn't fly twenty feet without stopping to rest. Instead, Barry used Prissy Measly's old owl, Herpes.

Then Barry went to Nigel's room in the still extravagantly roofless Grittyfloor Tower. Must get a team of contractor-wizards on this, Barry thought. Being open to the wet meant that the moisture was held in the walls; a Mumbling Mould had crept even to lower floors like this one. Getting on his hands and knees, he looked under his son's bed for his old mop. He'd given it to Nigel as soon as the wary acceptance letter had arrived. To his knowledge, Nigel had done nothing with it since, except apply a few decals. The Christmas before, Gramps Cringer had given Nigel a new model that was all the rage, but – in Barry's estimation – for posers, not players. But Nigel wouldn't be swayed; he loved his new mop, and named it Daisy.

He wasn't even planning to bring the old mop to school, but Barry had convinced him: 'You'll want the spare,' he had told Nigel. 'If your mop doesn't break at least once, you're not playing hard enough.'

Barry felt blindly. Something slick – a magazine? Something furry – a forgotten sandwich? But no mop.

'AHA!' said a familiar voice. 'Snooping around in rooms during classtime!' It was Peeves, Hogwash's most irritating ghost.

'Hi, Peeves,' Barry said coolly, sitting up.

'Don't you "hi" me, Trotter. You're stealing something – like to see you explain your way out of this one. It'll be fifty points from Grittyfloor and a good hiding—'

'You've had this coming for years, you sentient fart.' Barry leaned up, pointed his wand at Peeves and sent him straight to Hell.

'*Plotz*!' Barry intoned. Peeves howled as he was ripped apart by imps, each tiny being eating a piece, then shitting it out before Peeves's eyes (which were consumed last). Then each little piece of poo caught on fire and disappeared in a puff of acrid purple smoke.

'God! I've wanted to do that for ever,' Barry said. 'I've just been waiting for the proper moment . . . here it is,' he said, extracting the already dusty mop. Brushing it off, he walked over to the window. Balancing his haemorrhoid doughnut on the shaft (now he knew why they called Quiddit 'a young wizard's game'), he gingerly mounted the mop, then sped to the pitch. As he swooped down, he saw Nigel and the rest of the Grittyfloor team returning to the school, their mops over their shoulders.

'Where are you lads going?' Barry said jauntily. 'Can't expect to improve if you don't practise.'

'It's raining,' said the captain.

The sun was bright and there wasn't a cloud in the sky. Barry immediately suspected a scam from his school days. 'You, what's your name?'

'Mallory, sir.'

'Mallory, go and wake up Ferd and Jorge Measly and tell them to come out here. The rest of you, follow me.'

Barry shot straight up and the Grittyflavians followed; sure enough, five Silverfishers, led by Larval Malfeasance, had been pissing on the Grittyfloor squad from above. With a flick of his wand, Barry reversed the flow of their urine, sending it zooming backwards into their bladders, a very unpleasant sensation. Then he added the contents of the Grittyfloor team's bladders, too. The Silverfishers were suddenly ready to pop.

'Oldest trick in the book,' Barry said to the Grittyflavians. Below, he spied two more Silverfishers busily stuffing a Grittyfloor player through the goal. 'Hey you, what do you think you're doing?'

'Nuthin',' a hulking tow-headed kid said.

'"Nuthin',"' Barry mimicked, somehow managing to make it sound even more cretinous than the original. 'Clear off!'

'My dad always let us practise whenever we wanted,' said Larval, who had swooped down to join the fray. He was the Silverfish Sic'er.

'I can fix it so you spend a lot more time with him,' Barry said. 'Get lost.'

'Who's going to make us?' Larval said, dismounting and sloshing into fighting position.

Barry looked at his son, who was pale. 'Nigel,' he said, 'get off your mop. Wallop this wand-weasel.'

'But Mum said never to fight,' Nigel said, turning pale. A few people laughed.

'Mum's not here,' Barry said. 'Do it.'

Usually a lover of terra firma, Nigel dismounted reluctantly and took off his glasses, handing them to a fifth-year named Stevenson.

'If the worst happens, give these to my mother,' he said. Stevenson nodded. Then to his father, 'I can't see, Dad. You know I can't see.'

'Not fair using magic to help your kid,' somebody said to Barry.

'No magic,' Barry said. 'It'll be a fair fight. Nigel, you're on your own.'

As the teams crowded around them shouted encouragement, Nigel and Larval began circling each other. Larval came in, and socked Nigel right on the nose.

'Ahh!' The stabbing pain completely severed Nigel's brain from any sense of restraint. He immediately grabbed the pasty, smirking Larval's shirt, pulled him closer, then punched him in the stomach as hard as he could. In a hundred-to-one shot, Larval exploded, drenching everyone in urine.

The Grittyfloor squad mobbed Nigel, and carried on in a stinky, jubilant mass.

'Boys, let that be a lesson to you: never fight on a full bladder,' Barry said. 'Now Silverfishers, clear off.'

Sullenly picking up shreds of Malfeasance as they went, the Silverfishers reluctantly gave up the pitch.

Ferd and Jorge appeared presently, following a quick *Caffination* spell.

'No, the point of the game is *not* to help the other team catch the Sneetch,' Barry was explaining. 'Who told you that?'

'Larval,' said the Grittyfloor captain, whose simple-mindedness was exceeded only by his lack of coordination. Barry's response instantly turned him from captain into a scrub. He had been a Basher for six years, and had achieved renown by never once making contact, coming up with more and more baroque variations on the basic whiff.

'Hey, Barry,' Ferd said. 'What stinks?'

'Besides this team, you mean?' Barry said. 'Ask Nigel.'

'Well, nobody's born knowing how to play,' Jorge said. 'Except you, of course.' He saw Barry's doughnut. 'That is an excellent idea.' Jorge took out his wand. '*C'mere,*' he said, and an old lady in Surrey had an experience her children dismissed as senility.

'Shall I hit some fungoes to them?' Ferd said, getting out a Brainer.

'Sure,' Barry said. Two Bashers weren't paying any attention, laughing and hitting each other. 'You two! Stop! Since you want to hit something so badly, go with him,' Barry said, pointing to Ferd. 'He'll teach you how.'

'Since Woode's not here, I'll teach 'em goalkeeping,' Jorge said.[34]

[34] Oliver 'Morning' Woode had been Grittyfloor's legendary

'Everybody else, flying practice,' Barry said. 'Anybody who can touch me gets a Gallon.' He rocketed off, and the inexpert remnants wobbled after him.

Several hours later, Barry and his comrades were still whizzing to and fro.

'Can we please stop?' one Grittyfloor player asked. 'My bum's sore.'

'Yeah,' another said. 'We've missed nearly all of our morning classes.'

'Nice priorities,' Barry said. He was disgusted. '*I* didn't learn anything this morning, but you don't see me complaining.' In fact, his bottom was sore, too. Also, his back was stiffening up, he was losing circulation in his legs, his face was sizzling with wind burn – and his mop was binding him in a most uncomfortable way. Deciding that Ermine had probably finished whatever work she wanted him to help with, he decided to pack it in. 'All right,' he said. 'That's enough for today. But be here at seven a.m. sharp tomorrow. We're going to work on something I like to call, "the Crazy Ivan".'

Barry touched down to a chorus of groans. He was met by Professor Mumblemumble, who was carrying a

goalkeeper, and had to be put on suicide watch after every loss. Thanks to years of counselling, the love of his wife, Krista, and incredibly powerful meds, Woode now had a successful business selling magical athletic tape.

small plastic cup. The lengths of duct tape the professor used to fix his glasses over his balaclava were extra long today, and flapped a bit when he walked.

'Hello, Professor,' Barry said. 'Why aren't you teaching?'

'They can occupy themselves for a moment,' Mumblemumble lied. 'I saw you out here and brought you some Dragonade.'

'Thanks.' Barry drank some – it tasted strange, like photo-developing chemicals. It was so bad even his interrobang throbbed. 'Ick,' Barry said, 'I appreciate the gesture, but that stuff is strangely reminiscent of manticore piss.' He handed the cup back to Mumblemumble. 'And not in a good way.'

'I know,' Mumblemumble said, pouring it on the ground. The grass literally shrank back into the dirt rather than absorb it. 'Why do you think I never played Quiddit?'

Barry turned to the students. 'Team, when is the match against Silverfish?'

'In about two weeks,' the hapless captain said.

'That's not much time,' Barry said. To have any chance at the House Cup, they would have to beat Silverfish . . . which meant that they had no chance at all. 'Ferd, Jorge – I say it's time to teach these boys how to play Extreme Quiddit.'

'I was hoping you'd say that!' Ferd said. Jorge just cackled rather evilly.

'Remember Black Thursday?' Jorge said. One day during their first year, the entire Silverfish team had been slaughtered – the seldom-seen 'clean sweep' of Extreme Quiddit.

'All right,' Barry said. 'Starting tomorrow, we're going to teach you how to play like the big boys and girls. We're going to teach you how to ram, how to bind, how to shoot a gun from the saddle—'

'Always remember to lead 'em,' Jorge said.

'– how to drop chaff to short out a mop, how to use spikes, nets, piano wire, the whole thing.'

'But Headmister, isn't that cheating?' a Basher named Norval asked.

'Look, there are over seven hundred thousand different ways to cheat in Quiddit. Blogging, boinking, biatching – and none of 'em looks any different from playing the game legally. Extreme Quiddit is different. It's obviously wrong, and quite painful to watch,' Barry said. 'If you do it properly, you'll probably get pretty messy, and most of Silverfish's team will be killed, so decide now whether you have the stomach for it.'

The Grittyflavians cheered, giving their answer loud and clear. It didn't surprise Nigel that his dad was an impresario of cheating. As usual, pride and embarrassment were running neck and neck.

'However, you'll be banned from playing again this year and, if you're really good at it, maybe for ever.'

'All right with us,' one player said amid the smiles. 'I'm sick of taint-splinters.'

Barry's son was silent. 'Nigel? Now that you've exploded a man, any moral qualms?'

'No-o,' he said, 'but I don't think we should tell Mum.'

'Then it's settled,' Barry said. 'Tomorrow morning, we'll start.'

'On three, everybody,' Ferd said. '"Death from Above." One, two, three!'

There was a final cheer, and everybody began straggling up the hill.

On the way back to the school, Mumblemumble told Barry about how he was having the students make powerful Dork hexes by cutting folded paper.

'Muddles think they're snowflakes – then they get eyebrow cancer!' Mumblemumble said. Barry was impressed; this Mumblemumble clearly knew his stuff.

Later that day, Nigel was sitting in the Grittyfloor Common Room, puzzling over his Latin. It was very difficult – you had to read through the whole spell to find the verb, which was usually the last place you looked. Yesterday in class, he conjured a *paella* instead of a *puella,* and had to treat everyone to lunch. The Yiddish was easier – when in doubt, clear your throat – but there was less of it.

To his immense relief, Nigel had found himself far from the only non-magical first-year at Hogwash. When Dorco became Headmister, he and Ludicrous had pushed through a plan whereby Muddle students could participate in a special 'Wizard, Last-Class' certificate programme. It was horrifically expensive, and utterly useless, and so became the in-thing among the Muddle rich and well-connected. In fact, the Trustees discovered that the more outrageous the price, the more applicants they ended up with. Muddle money was not only paying for the theme park, it was also funding a new extension to the Malfeasance home.

Of course it was slightly different for Nigel. People expected him to have magic spewing out of his ears, and when he didn't they started to tease him. But the taser his dad had given him to ward off overzealous fans worked as well as any spell, and Junior was always quick with a comeback if he was around when Nigel's mojo went missing. And now that he had popped Larval, people treated him with a certain kind of respect bordering on fear.

'Oh, fewmets,' Nigel said, looking at the clock on the wall. He would have to hurry if he was going to make it to his next class, the only one he really liked. It was called Making Sense of Muddles, and it was taught by Author Measly.

Back when he was Headmister, Lon Measly had hired his father to teach a course on Muddles (and walk him occasionally). Tenure was a force even Dork magic couldn't sweep away, not without stirring up the Magical Teachers' Union, and so Author Measly stayed put. Ludicrous's recent visit had been tough on him, but Measley had given as good as he got; anyway, a split lip and a black eye still in full flood did not diminish his eloquence, or his enthusiasm for his topic.

'Welcome back, class. I trust you all have been reading your Muddle newspapers. Has anyone figured out what the Muddles are fighting over?' Measly said. He scanned the class for hands. 'No one? Well, don't feel so bad, I haven't been able to figure it out either. Keep reading, though – perhaps one of you students will be the one to decipher this great sphincter.'[35]

Measly opened his lecture notes. 'Let's start with a

[35] The sphincter was a mythical beast, a cross between a sphinx and a cipher. Winston Churchill once called Josef Stalin 'a sphincter wrapped inside a riddle wrapped inside an enigma'. Actually he didn't, but he *could have*.

quick refresher. A Muddle is a creature that looks like a witch or wizard, but is completely without the ability to harness magic; in the direst of cases, Muddles cannot even perceive magic.'

I wish, Nigel thought, and began an ambitious programme of doodling.

Professor Measly looked up. 'Now, is there anyone who has never met a Muddle?'

A hand shot up.

'Ah. Glad I asked. Doubtless you grew up in an all-magical commune?'

'Yes, Professor,' a Pufnstuf named Panacea Pangloss said.

'Against them, myself,' Measly said. 'Like war, living with Muddles is wonderfully broadening – and as I've said, you can't have the one without the other. Even the most simple, blinkered, irritating of creatures has something to teach us. Remember that.

'Anyway, quickly –' The professor made a swipe or two with his wand, and a doughy woman in a flowered dress appeared on stage. She had been sitting on a chair, and immediately collapsed in a heap when she arrived but the furniture did not.

'What the—?'

'Pardon me, madam,' Professor Measly said, looking

down at her. 'You were transported here for educational purposes. Say "hello".'

'H-hello?' the poor woman said.

'Thank you!' Measly sang. He waved his wand again, and she disappeared with a pop.

'Now, Pangloss, you've met a Muddle. Feel broadened?'

'Yes, Professor. Thank you.'

'Good.' He continued reading from his notes. 'Though some scholars were convinced that Muddles were physically different from wizards – that they were in fact a different species altogether, Neanderthals to our Homo Sapiens – in my view this is incorrect. Muddles are identical to you and me. But, being unmagical, they simply refuse to acknowledge the presence of magic.'

A hand was raised. 'All of them?' a boy asked.

'Up until recently,' Professor Measly replied. 'Before the Trotter books, the less a Muddle acknowledged magic – even though it might be happening right in front of his eyes, constantly – the more intelligent he would be considered by his peers.'

A mumble of disapproval rolled through the class. Somebody said 'Stupid cows!' under their breath.

The professor heard it. 'Now, now, we mustn't judge. We must try to understand – then judge,' he said.

Nigel considered pointing out that Muddles generally had better teeth than wizards, but decided against it.

'Take this Muddle device, for example,' Professor Measly said, picking up a television remote from his desk. 'When a Muddle points this at the television set—'

The commune girl's hand raised again. 'Excuse me, sir, what's a television?'

'A lot like your family's recreational scrying set,' the professor said. 'It doesn't seem to be able to predict the future, even though there's a button here clearly marked, "fast-forward" . . .' The professor was annoyed by this inconsistency.

'It's important to keep in mind that we are constantly finding out more about Muddles, and revising accordingly. Some scholars who have watched television believe that it is purely entertainment, but I myself believe it is a type of hypnosis, or possibly punishment. Anyway, when a Muddle points this thing – which is obviously a primitive wand – the television springs to life. But the Muddle does not call it magic. They insist that the wand emits some sort of ray. No one has ever seen any of these rays, or smelled one, or tasted one. I believe that your average Muddle – which is very average indeed – understands how preposterous this explanation is, because they couldn't care less. And yet those Muddles with enough curiosity to wonder why this device works are so shackled with anti-magic prejudice that any other explanation will do.'

'Are rays the only explanations that Muddles have?' Junior asked.

The professor laughed. 'No, no – the lengths to which a Muddle will go to deny magic are quite amazing; when confronted with levitation, they will call it "aerodynamics". There's "chemistry", "physics", "electricity" – none of which you can see, or hold in your hand, or collect in a bucket. It would be funny, if they weren't so anxious to force their ignorance on any wizard that tries to teach them the truth.' The professor pointed to a scar on his knuckle. 'I got this in a friendly discussion of prestidigitation at a Muddle pub, while gathering material for a research paper.'

'Will *none* of them believe in magic?' a student asked in exasperation.

'That is a bit more complex than you might guess,' Measly said. 'When Muddles are young – especially now, after the Trotter books have revealed our world to them – many of them *do* believe in magic.' The Professor said. 'Or at least in the possibility that Muddles do not already know *everything* worth knowing. But the adults are different. None of them say they believe in magic, not if they want to stay out of the loony-bin,' Measly said. 'Those who cannot ignore the vast amount of things they cannot explain don't usually call it magic. They call it "religion", and use it as a reason to kill each other.'

'How barbaric,' a Grittyfloor student not important enough to the plot to receive a name said.

'Quite so,' Measly said.

'Why don't we force them to understand?' a similarly luckless Silverfisher asked.

'We could, but what for? It would be very time consuming, and wouldn't profit us a bit. The same argument has been made for exterminating them.'

A hand went down. 'That idea comes up every so often,' Measly said. 'I'm against it. Sentimental, I suppose. And I, personally, find them hysterically funny. Now class, will you open your texts to page forty-four. Here we see the Muddles' laughable ideas about their own reproduction. Note that fairies play no role whatsoever . . .'

Class was fun. Professor Measly would show a Muddle artefact, and describe what it was used for, which he always got spectacularly wrong. Matches were called 'torches', and toothpicks were described as 'biodegradable devices to get someone's attention unobtrusively'. By the time a handgun was rolled out – as 'an amazingly efficient way to punch holes in paper' – Nigel could take no more.

He raised his hand. 'Professor?'

'Yes, Trotter?'

'I don't think that's quite right,' Nigel said.

'What do you mean?' the professor said, as the class tittered.

'Your analysis,' Nigel said. 'I don't think that's what guns are used for.'

'Of course it is. Look for yourself. Here, Broadbottom, hold this.' The Professor tossed a book to a student in the front row, Cyril Broadbottom.[36]

'For God's sake, Broadbottom, stop *wiggling*,' Measly took aim, then shot. He plucked the paper from the sprawled Cyril, who gave a slight moan. 'Just wipe some of this blood away . . . See?' He flipped through the book. 'A perfect hole on every page. It is a cunning non-magical solution to an age-old problem.'

'It's just that my grandparents are Muddles,' Nigel said. 'And they always use a hole-punch.'

'Your grandparents are clearly weirdoes,' Professor Measly said with growing annoyance.

Nigel hadn't twigged. 'But, Professor!'

[36] Named for his Uncle Cyril, who had been inadvertently killed by Zed Grimfood during Barry's eleventh year.

'Enough, Trotter.' Nigel reluctantly shut up. 'If I say it is used for punching holes, then that is what it is used for!'

After class was over, Nigel went up to Professor Measly's desk. 'Professor, may I speak to you for a moment?'

'You look just like Barry,' Professor Measly said. 'Bet I'm the first person ever to say that,' he added drily.

'Barry who?' Nigel said, one-upping him.

'And cheeky like him, too.' Measly laughed, but Nigel just smiled, unsure and nervous after their earlier set-to.

Measly continued to gather up his papers. 'You're mighty confident for a first-year,' he said. 'You might want to watch that. Any other professor would've taken five points from Grittyfloor for your outburst.'

'I'm sorry,' Nigel said. 'It's just that—'

'Oh, I know what a gun is really for, my lad,' Measly said. 'But I don't think the entire class has to know it yet. Better for them to think of Muddles as harmless morons or Barry Trotter wanna-bes for a few more years. Then they can find out the bad news . . . What can I do for you? Are you getting on all right?' the professor said.

'Actually, sir, I'd like to speak with you in private, if possible.'

Measly's face grew more serious, matching Nigel's expression. 'Certainly, certainly – can I ask what this is about?'

Nigel blushed and looked down for a moment. 'I'd rather not talk about it here, if you don't mind. It's . . . I'd just rather not.'

'All right,' the professor said, somewhat perplexed. 'Come to my office.'

Measly's office looked like nothing so much as a particularly squalid Muddle junk shop. Objects of all shapes and sizes, most rusted, bent, dinged or dusty, packed the small room. Measly's days were spent plucking an object at random, then trying to divine its function through trial and error. He copied down any 'discoveries' in a leather-bound notebook. Nigel saw that there were fifty of them, at least. And he had no doubt that they were all completely wrong.

As soon as the door closed, before either of them had even had a chance to sit down, Nigel blurted out, 'I'm not magical.'

Professor Measly laughed.

'You may think it's funny, but it's very serious to me!' Nigel said.

'I'm sure it is, I just find that very hard to believe,' the Professor said. 'Look at your parents.'

'Don't remind me!'

'You don't get along with them too well?'

'No,' Nigel said. 'Mostly because they like my sister better. She's magical as all hell.'

The profanity was no surprise to Measly. He was around children enough to know how they talked and, as Hogwash's designated 'cool teacher', heard much worse.

'I'm sure your parents love you just the way you are,' Professor Measly said. 'I mean, I love Lonald, and he once dated a girl simply because she smelled like hamburger.' He toyed with a rusty coathanger. 'Anyway, Nigel, being magical isn't an all-or-nothing proposition.'

'What do you mean?' Nigel said.

'I mean that everybody's magical to a greater or lesser degree. Occasionally, somebody will come along who has a natural talent for it, somebody like your father. But for most of us, it's a question of developing what we have to the fullest,' the professor said. 'Each of us has a special energy called "wha?". "Wha?" is sort of like confusion, or impulsiveness. That's where the magic comes from, in part. Your father is a very impulsive, very confused person. That's why he's a great – well, I use "great" loosely – wizard.'

'But my mum, she's not confused. She's just the opposite,' Nigel said. 'She sneaks into my room and organises my spare change.'

'"Wha?" is only half the story. Magic also requires great desire. You want food, money, or anything else intensely enough, and that focuses your "wha?" into magic,' Professor Measly said. 'Your father has the worst impulse control I've ever seen in a non-psychotic. Your mother is the most desirous – lusty – person I've ever met. See, it all fits.'

Nigel knitted his brow. 'I suppose I don't know much about magic,' he said. His familiar sloshed slightly at his waist – the water was murky, he ought to change it. He felt a comforting tentacle brush his belt buckle.

'I like your choice in familiars,' Measly said. 'I once wrote an excellent song about an octopus. It's called "Anorak of the Deep". They're—'

'– as smart as house cats, I know,' Nigel said.

Professor Measly got out a lute, and began to play and sing in a good, but fruity voice. Being around singing people always embarrassed Nigel for some reason, so he asked the first question that popped into his head.

'So what's the difference between good magic and Dork magic?'

Professor Measly stopped playing for a moment. 'Soul,' he said, and started playing again.

'What's that supposed to mean?' Nigel asked. The teacher stopped again.

'It's hard to say. Loving people more than things is a big part of it. So is not being afraid, or at least not doing everything *because* you're afraid.' He put his lute down. 'Treating other people as you would have them treat you goes a long way.'

'That seems a bit obvious, Professor,' Nigel said.

'Oh, now it's not enough for you for something to be right,' the professor said. 'Now it's got to be entertaining, too.'

'No,' Nigel said. 'Just that it seems too easy.'

Professor Measly leaned over his desk, and looked at Nigel, considering. The boy suddenly felt very pale and short and schlumpy. 'You ever been a Boy Scout?' he asked.

'No – well, yeah. For about three hours.' One of the few times something magical had happened around Nigel was when a bowl of punch had turned into blood. Nigel wasn't sure if he had done it or not – but somebody *had* just made fun of his neckerchief.

'Only three hours?' the professor said. 'Then you

know how hard it is to be noble, wise, brave, kind, clean, courteous and all that jazz all the time. Good magic – I hesitate to use the term "white" magic, for obvious reasons,' the professor said with a smile, 'comes from the good parts of ourselves. Dork magic happens when we're not acting as we ought to – when we're being stupid or selfish or greedy or mean.'

Nigel considered this.

'So does that answer your question?' Professor Measly said. 'You seem puzzled.'

'I'm trying to figure out what kind of wizard my dad is,' Nigel said.

Professor Measly laughed. 'Both, obviously! We're all both!'

Nigel fixed the professor with a look. 'Do you know some of the pranks Dad did?'

'Oh, yes,' the professor said. 'Remember, Lon was along for most of it! I know your father well. There's a lot of mischief in him – like there is in Ferd and Jorge – but at heart, he's good.'

The professor looked at his watch. 'I've talked too long!' He showed it to Nigel. 'Have you ever seen one of these?' he asked. 'Neat Muddle gizmo. It tells you what time it is. Some of them even show you what day it is. Much more convenient than rushing outside and looking at the sun or stars. Works when it's cloudy!' Professor Measly laughed.

Nigel got up. 'Yeah, I've seen it, it's called a watch.'

'That's right, that's right,' the professor said. 'I mean, don't get me wrong, our wizard clocks have their uses, even if they tell you things you'd rather not know.' Professor Measly had one above his desk which gave the current activities of each of the members of his family; its hands were pointing to things like 'tarting about with Rockhard', 'embezzling from G'ingots' and 'licking oneself'. He walked over to the door to let Nigel out.

As Nigel got to the door, he spied a pamphlet that had been framed; it was signed, 'To Author, from Mo – the best fight is one you avoid. But if you can't . . .'

The professor noticed Nigel looking at it. 'Ever heard of Gandhi?' Measly said. 'Very great non-violent wizard. He's a hero of mine.'

Nigel read the cover aloud. '"Mr Knee, Meet Mr Nuts: A Thousand and One Dirty Tricks to Win Any Fight, From the Barroom to the Boardroom and Beyond."' Nigel sniffed. 'Doesn't seem non-violent to me. And you don't either.'

'I don't? Why not?' Nigel pointed to his eye and lip.

'Oh, right. Well,' – Professor Measly opened the door and Nigel ducked under the flap of his white robes

– 'just because a person wants to be non-violent, that doesn't mean he can't kick somebody's arse a little in self-defence. Anyway, you should talk – we all heard what you did to Larval Malfeasance.' Professor Measly showed a clenched fist. 'Right on!' he whispered, eyes twinkling.

Nigel laughed, and they shook hands. For that moment at least, he felt at home among the wizards of Hogwash.

Chapter Nine

THE PERILS OF POMMEFRITTE

As Professor Measly explained the facts of magical life to their son, Barry sat in his office playing solitaire on his scrying bowl and Ermine worked. He felt a tickle in his throat. By dinnertime he was feeling distinctly nauseous.

'I told you not to walk through the kitchens,' Ermine said. 'What you don't know can't kill your appetite. Anyway, a little house elf spit never hurt anybody.'

'I think I've got flu or something, though that does make me feel even worse,' Barry said. 'Why do we even give them jobs?'

'Strong union,' Ermine said.

That evening at dinner, Barry only made it halfway through the appetisers before rushing off to vomit. As he passed, Madame Sprig politely asked him if he wouldn't mind doing that on the compost heap. 'Every little helps!' she said, but Barry wasn't in a position to reply. He completed his necessary errand and went straight to bed.

The next morning, he felt just as bad – he showed it by not shaving – but went to Quiddit practice anyway.

'Oliver would be proud,' Ermine said, slapping him on the back heartily.

'Please don't touch me,' Barry said. 'Even my hair hurts.'

'All right, dear,' Ermine said, blowing a kiss. 'Have a good day.'

Barry smiled weakly. As he walked to the pitch, he weaved slightly – whatever bug he had caught could certainly pack a punch.

Being airborne turned out to be an even worse idea, and Barry booted copiously. Eventually the Measlys positioned him above, and made the Sic'ers try to manoeuvre each other so they got hit. It was unorthodox, but seemed to be working; after an hour, the Grittyfloor team was improving. Then came explosives practice, and learning how to garrotte the opposing goalkeeper with piano wire. Finally, they all learned how to dive out of the sun, and the Measly twins pronounced them done.

'That's enough for today,' Ferd said. 'As you're walking around school, I'd like you to imagine scenes of indescribable carnage and suffering, peopled by the Silverfish Quiddit team.'

'That's right,' Jorge said. 'This sort of thing doesn't come easy to us wizards, but with a little practice you can be as bloody-minded and remorseless as any Muddle. Trust us, you'll need it once the bodily fluids start to flow.' The team listened intently; Barry was retching noisily a short distance away. 'You only have a certain number of fouls before the game is forfeited, so every foul must disable an opponent. Tomorrow, we use the sand-filled socks.'

After a rousing cheer, they all tromped off for a shower in the school's execrable athletic facilities. In addition to sentient athlete's foot, the showers were filled with the Radishgnaw Wizard Water Polo[37] team. To let it clear out – and to avoid questions about when the school planned to pay an exterminator to clear the pool of mer-junkies (they had colonised it during the vacant summer months) – Barry sat in the steam room with Zed Grimfood, who had just had a beard massage.

[37] Wizard water polo is somewhat like our version, except each player levitates above the water, with only a single toe sticking in. Their movements create ripple patterns like a Zen garden. If they disturb the surface of the water too much, they receive a penalty. The game is played with a creature similar to a tribble, only more waterlogged and much less happy.

Zed sat there, naked, very hairy and red. He was thinking of buying some property, and couldn't decide whether to do it in this dimension, or another one.

'You've done pretty well, haven't you?' he asked.

'Yeah, I think so,' Barry said.

'What did you pay?' Zed asked.

'Uhhh . . .' Barry couldn't remember. As Zed asked more questions, Barry realised he couldn't remember anything about his home, not even the address.

'If you didn't want to talk about it . . .' Zed grumbled, and walked out of the room.

'Stop staring at my bahookie, nancyboy,' Barry heard him mutter.

After his shower, Barry went to the Great Hall for breakfast. Ermine was finishing her column for the week. 'Want one?' she said, proffering a bagel. 'According to the package, they're "Kabbala-riffic".'

'If it's food, I don't want it,' Barry said. 'I'm here for some juice then I'm back to bed.'

Going to get a glass, he stood in line behind some third-years from Pufnstuf.

'Omigod, Headmister Trotter' – the sound of this still charmed Barry like a particularly tickling obscenity – 'can I just say that seeing your movies was, like, the biggest thrill for me?' one said. 'Until I got into Hogwash.'

'Thank you,' Barry said. 'They weren't really my movies, they were—'

'Like when you saved that guy!' she said.

'Yeah, that was great,' another student concurred.

'Do you really have hair on your feet?' the first one said.

'No, I – well, a little, but—'

'Is that the Ring?' the second one asked.

'No, that's my wedding—listen, I think you might have me confused—'

'Then when you killed the Green Goblin,' the first one said.

Now Barry had no idea who they thought he was. Spiderman? 'But I—'

'Oh, I know you didn't mean to, but it was still cool,' the second one said. 'Anyway, we're glad you're Headmister, and not some old dried-up git.'

'Yeah! Not some clapped-out old pervert!'

'Yeah! My mum said that Bumblemore used to grab her boobs!'

'Sounds about right,' Barry said.

'Bye!' they said, and continued on to class.

'Let me perform a quick anti-stupidity incantation on

them,' said Professor Mumblemumble, who happened to be walking by.

'Be my guest, if you think it will help,' Barry said, turning to walk to his quarters and bed. A few quick phrases, a flash of blue-green lightning, and two piles of powder, a novelty pencil-topper and a scrap of satchel reading 'Chatterjee' sat where the students had stood.

Barry itched himself awake the next morning, prodded into consciousness by hundreds of tiny little hairs littering his pillow. He sat up, and a few longer ones spilled from between the buttons of his birthday pyjamas. (The pyjamas were ridiculous looking, but even in mid-September Hogwash was too draughty for such quibbling.) He looked down and saw the hairs. His heart skipped a beat and he checked his head – no, it was all there; in fact, there seemed to be *more* of it. Barry was composing his testimonial to the hair tonic he spilled in the bath when he happened to rub his jaw. It was completely smooth. That's odd, Barry thought. And of course he still felt like Death was camping in his mouth – but what disease made you clean-shaven?

Ermine, who had been woken up to receive accusations of shaving her legs in bed, was adamant. 'I'm taking you to see Nurse Pommefritte.'

'But Erm, she's a butcher. She's an over-ambitious vet.'

'No arguments. And stop overreacting,' Ermine said, pulling on some clothes and wetting down her hair. Ermine had enough hair for two people, possibly three, Barry thought with irritation.

'No, really,' he said. 'People have died.'

'Don't worry, I'll make sure the big, bad nurse doesn't stick you with a needle, ickle Barry.'

'Or give me a dog's brain!'

'Lon would've been a vegetable without Nurse Pommefritte,' Ermine said.

'So now he's an animal instead.'

'Better than a mineral,' she replied. The set of her jaw demonstrated to Barry that the discussion phase was over, so he allowed himself to be taken to the infirmary. As usual, the school was ravaged by mono. Nurse Pommefritte had spent a great deal of time and money on an education campaign designed to discourage the kissing of doorknobs, toilet seats and other unsavoury locations. But everything – even the daily leaflets dropped by hundreds of owls – was for naught. Useless against disease, the garish, unsettling propaganda only made Barry consider swearing off all physical contact, and stoked poor Nigel's hypochondria no end. (He and the nurse were already on a first-name basis.)

In the strengthening light, Barry and Ermine made their way to Hogwash's medical wing. This was, of course, wing-shaped. It looked rather odd from the outside, but was relatively normal from the inside, allowing for a slight tendency to flap in the breeze.

Puppy Pommefritte had begun her career at the Hogsbleede Uncomfortable Place for the Extremely Naughty, and it was clear that she considered painful medical care to be part of the punishment for the bad judgement or moral failing that resulted in the injury itself. In addition to various gleaming, pointed implements, the mere possession of which constituted a human rights violation, the walls of her office were crammed with pictures of Nurse Pommefritte and the leading lights of the magical world, all of whom she had treated. And, Barry noticed, all of whom paid an awful price for that association.

'I didn't know that Cornelius Grunge had bats' wings for ears,' Barry said.

'Yes,' Ermine said. 'That's why he started wearing his hair long. You know, "the grunge look".'

'I thought he was just a trendy. Can he fly?'

'Enough to get about an inch off the ground,' Ermine said. 'They're mostly ornamental. Otherwise the Ministry would force him to get a pilot's licence.'

Ermine saw a photo of Barry's godfather Serious,

sporting four Swiss Army knife-like attachments where his fingers used to be. There was a corkscrew, a nail file, a retractable fish-measuring ruler . . . It was, in a word, handy. 'Have you seen Serious lately?' Ermine asked. 'What's the deal with his hand?'

'Some friends of Lord Valumart called in their loan,' Barry said. 'As far as I know, he's still trying to sell those "Kitchen Wizard" things to Muddles.' This was a sort of enchanted Cuisinart, hawked on late-night TV. It was useful enough, but had a tendency to go insane and slaughter its owners which Serious couldn't always laugh off, cover up or explain away. Instead he offered a 'Lifetime Guarantee', without making it clear that it was the purchaser's lifetime, not the Kitchen Wizard's. In the wizarding world, there was no concept of 'negligent homicide'. This benefited Nurse Pommefritte as well.

'Good morning!' the nurse said cheerily as she walked in. Barry hastily stuffed the pamphlet on Gonocadabra he had been reading into his pocket. Apparently, as long as your trouser elf was still visible, you were okay.

'Get on the table, Headmister.' Barry did so. 'So, the job wearing you down already?' she asked brusquely. 'Open your mouth.' Looking down his throat, she asked, 'Are you pregnant?'

Barry was flabbergasted. 'No, I'm a—'

'You're a wizard is what you are, and wizards' bodies are as nutty as their heads,' the nurse said. The old girl was all business. 'Any food cravings? Darkening of the nipples?'

'I honestly haven't looked.' Barry glanced at Ermine. 'Darling?'

'Don't drag me into this,' his wife said with a smile. 'I've got enough to do without tracking the state of your nipples. I'm going outside to read a magazine.'

'But you said you'd—' She was gone.

Pommefritte continued to poke and prod. 'Any morning sickness?'

'What's that again?' Barry asked.

'You know, throwing up in the mornings,' she said.

'I did that yesterday,' Barry said.

'Aha!' Nurse Pommefritte said.

'But I've been doing it fairly constantly lately . . .'

'Headmister, you really must let me do my job.' There was a tap on the door. 'Yes?'

A pretty young nurse with curly hair stuck her head in. 'Morning, Headmister. Nurse Pommefritte, Cyril Broadbottom says he's lost a testicle.'

'Cyril? He must be forty by now!' Barry exclaimed.

'It's his nephew,' the nurse said, to Barry's secret relief. His record was safe.

'I won't be a moment,' Nurse Pommefritte said to the nurse. 'Wait outside.'

Barry, thinking to his horror that the diagnosis of pregnancy would stand, vigorously began explaining his symptoms; he was determined to have his day in court. '. . . and then this morning,' Barry said, 'when I woke up, all my facial hair was gone.'

Nurse Pommefritte took a rusty scalpel down from the wall, and began to finger it. Luckily for Barry, this was simply a nervous habit.

'Hmm. You seem to be experiencing some sort of youthanasia,' Nurse Pommefritte said. Barry gave her a puzzled look.

'Getting younger,' she said. 'Have you been washing your hands? Chewed your food once per tooth? Eaten anything that screamed?'

'As much as ever, of course not, and no,' Barry answered.

'Have you made fun of any powerful wizards?'

'Only for the last twenty years,' Barry said. 'What does that have to do with anything?'

'Could be a hex, a curse – or a potion, which would mean it's out of my bailiwick,' she said. 'Snipe would have to handle that. And if you don't get any better in the next few days, I would see him immediately.'

'Why?' Barry said. 'I like watching my hair grow back.'

'Because if you don't arrest the progress of this disease, or hormone condition, or whatever it is that you've picked up, you'll continue to get younger and younger until you reach the age of zero.'

'I don't like the sound of that,' Barry said. 'What happens then?'

'You wink out like a candle,' Nurse Pommefritte said. 'I've never seen it, but I've heard it's very painful.' She went to a cupboard and got out a few vials; one contained pills, the other two viscous liquids that made Barry's stomach somersault on instinct alone. Barry remembered that cupboard well. He and the Measlys had once had a nice side business stealing controlled substances from there and selling them to other students. The side benefit was that everybody suspected that Bumblemore was a junkie; but after the Ministry started cracking down on the centaurs in the Forsaken Forest, Barry and his pals had had to cool it.

'This is geezerwort,' Nurse Pommefritte said, holding up a vial. 'Take two drops in tea, twice daily. And this is kidsbane; halve the dosage if you get less popular with the students. Let's try this for a few weeks. Then, if there's no improvement, I'll write you a prescription for an inhaler.'

'An inhaler?' Barry said.

'Old farts,' the nurse said. 'Strongest remedy I know.'

'And what are these?' Barry shook out a little pink pill from a vial. It had a circle with a line through it.

'Those are just in case you're pregnant,' she said.

'I AM NOT PREGNANT!' Barry said angrily.

'Headmister, everybody's a little pregnant.' There was clearly no arguing. 'Good day.'

Ermine came back into the room. 'Well?' she said.

'I'm getting younger,' Barry said.

'Yahoo!' Ermine said. 'You call the babysitter, I'll get the coconut-scented heat-up love oil!' She did a little hip-centric dance of lasciviousness.

'It's not good news,' Barry said.

'Why not?'

'Because if it doesn't stop, I'll get to zero and wink out,' he said.

'Oh no,' Ermine said. 'I've heard that's really painful.'

Barry put his clothes back on. 'I knew it,' he said glumly.

'Knew what?' Ermine said.

'It's Snipe,' he said, tying his purple wingtips with the toes that curled up at the ends. Now that he was Headmister, tradition dictated he dress like a waiter at a medieval theme restaurant. 'He's always wanted to be

Headmister. First he killed Dorco, and now he's put a spell on me.'

'You always say that, but this time I'm inclined to agree. They're always saying it at the zoology department, but I never really understood until now,' Ermine said, as they walked back to the Headmister's Office.

'What's that?' Barry said.

'The politics in academia are murder.'

Over the next several days, Barry improved, but only just. He was still unaging, but less quickly. After a week, however, it was clear that Nurse Pommefritte's remedies weren't going to save him.

'So now we go to Snipe,' Ermine said. 'Maybe if we ask him nicely . . .'

'No way, Ermine! That would be like signing my own death warrant!' Barry said. 'This time tomorrow, I'll be trading recipes with Dorco!'

'What did you call him last night? "Invisibugger"?'

'Mr Chilly-Britches,' Barry said.

Ermine sighed. This old feud was tiresome. 'So what do you think we should do?

'I think *you* should look for a cure,' Barry said. 'Come on, Ermine. You loved digging through old spell books way back when.'

'True, but what if I can't find a cure?' she said.

'Then we go to Snipe. But only as a last resort.'

'Barry, are you sure this is how you want to do it?' Ermine asked. 'Why don't we call Terry Valumart? You could use his personal physician.'

'Oh, my God . . .' Barry said. 'I never thought of that. Maybe Valumart's the one behind it?'

Ermine was dubious. 'I don't think—'

'No, listen: regardless of how much my next worst-seller saves him, I'm worth much more to Valumart dead than alive – think of the television retrospectives, the commemorative crap – hell, if I were him, I'd kill me!' he said with a dark chuckle.

'I don't know, Barry,' Ermine said.

Her husband pressed the point. It didn't matter that he was arguing for his own imminent (and probably painful) demise, it only mattered that she admitted he was right. 'Nothing comes between Terry and his bank balance. Did you know that whenever Terry comes over to the house, he always swipes something of mine and then sells it on eBuy? I only noticed because my collection of peekaboo pens was listed.'

'Peekaboo pens?'

'You tip one and the witch's clothes disappear,' Barry said. 'Or the mummy's wrappings.'

'Serves you right for looking yourself up on eBuy. You're too vain.'

'Wait a bit and you won't have to worry about it any more,' Barry said, fishing for sympathy. He really didn't feel all that bad. 'You'll be selling my stuff there to pay for school for Nigel and wossname.' He hadn't been able to remember his daughter's name all day.

'Her name is Fiona! Just because she's staying with my parents for a while, that's no excuse to cut her out of the family! Some father you are, Barry Trotter.'

'Sorry, Erm,' Barry said. 'I honestly forgot. I think my brain might be getting younger, too.'

Energised by her outburst, Ermine barked out a plan. 'Okay, here's how it's going to be: first, we're going to ask every teacher here if they know how to cure you.'

'Even Snipe?' Barry said.

'Especially Snipe,' Ermine said. 'But since you're such a coward, we'll ask him last. Then, if nobody knows, I'll hit the Hogwash Library and we'll do research together.'

'Oh, the Library,' Barry groused. 'That'll be a laugh and a half.'

Ermine paid no attention. 'You need to write everything down somewhere, so after you forget it you can re-learn it,' she said. 'Get Lon to help. Then, after you're cured, we're going to find out which magical fuckwit did this to you, and put the "grim" back in grimoire. Got it?'

There was no denying Ermine in this mood – nor did Barry have a sensible alternative. 'Fine, dear,' he said meekly. But old habits of work-avoidance die hard. 'I'll need to conserve my energy [cough, cough],' Barry said, playing his illness for all it was worth. 'Can I hire some secretaries? To help? Just three or four? And of course they'd have to be in top physical condition . . .'

Ermine shot him a sceptical look. '*Right*. You may be getting younger, but I'm not getting stupid.'

'Okay, forget it. I'll write my memoirs myself.' Once again the foul spectre of toil appeared. 'I'll dictate them. To Lon, like you said. He'll help me remember.'

And so Plan A was set into motion, with owls stencilled 'Personal and Confidential' sent to all departments. Surely someone would know a cure, and if they didn't there was always Plan B, Ermine doing what she was born to do, reading stuff and getting everybody into a lot of trouble as a result.

'Cheer up, Bar,' Ermine said. 'You can always torture Ponce.'

'Erm, that is an *excellent* idea,' Barry said. An owl was sent to the Measly twins for inspiration.

Chapter Ten
THE SLEUTHING BEGINS

Over the next few days, Barry and Ermine grilled the teaching staff. Or tried to – something always seemed to happen that prevented them from getting any information. First Professor Sprig was hauled off to jail after an anonymous tip led police to massive quantities of marijuana in the Hogwash greenhouses. 'I use it to give the fly-traps appetite,' drawled the ever-woozy Herbology professor. 'The argusberry bush has glaucoma!'

Then, as he was composing a reply to Barry and Ermine's owl, Professor Bunns was informed that he must become a member of the Ghostly Teachers' Union. Twenty years behind in dues, Bunns left immediately to find higher-paying work.

The same day, tiny, robotic Professor Flipswitch fell in love with the school's toaster; the pair eloped to Morocco, where 'we can live together as man and wife with dignity'. Even Barry's follow-up appointment with Nurse Pommefritte was abruptly cancelled, after a mysterious outbreak of Creeping Swahili.

Barry and Ermine did talk to Madame Cootch, but the poor woman had been concussed so many times the conversation soon veered into her favourite topic, 'that funny ringing sound'.

'Do you hear it?' she asked, for the umpteenth time.

'Nope,' Barry and Ermine answered again.

Afterwards, back in the Headmister's Office, Ermine turned to Barry and said, 'I think we need to ask Snipe for help.'

'No, Ermine,' Barry said. 'He's the guy behind it in the first place.'

'Barry, nobody respects your right to be stupidly fixated on Snipe more than I do, but it always turns out to be Valumart,' Ermine said. 'Think of all the time you would've saved over your career if you'd asked Snipe for help immediately. And right now, time is exactly what you *don't* have.'

'I'd prefer not to,' Barry said, and turned away, his arms folded.

'Very mature,' Ermine said. 'I'm going to, and you can't stop me.' She wrote out a note, stuck a Post-It marked 'Urgent' on the owl's head, and waited for a response.

It never came. Even as Mitey the owl was winging across the school, Hogwash's redoubtable Professor of Notions was in a pair of aura-cuffs, being led out of his dank, creepy, quilt-filled office by Muddle policemen. The story came out over the next few days in the *Daily Soothsayer*: apparently Snipe had been caught in an amateur sting operation run by underage girls posing as hard-bitten undercover policemen. Snipe's scrying bowl, hidden among his piles of unwholesome stitchery, was confiscated, and thousands of images of grubby, middle-aged cops in compromising positions were unearthed. Clearly Snipe had been too preoccupied to poison Barry.

'With a predator like him out of scryberspace,' said the early edition of the *Stun*, 'police officers everywhere can sleep better at night. We all owe the enterprising Lolitas a debt of gratitude.'

'Disgusting,' Barry said. When he looked at the picture, Snipe covered his face with his manacled hands. 'I've said it before: never trust a man who does macrame.'

'So what do we do now?' Ermine said. 'I vote for talking to Terry.' They called, but even the Dork Lord provided an airtight alibi.

'Nobody knows this, but I failed Latin,' Valumart admitted. 'Never been able to make heads or tails of the bloody language.'

'Wow, that's quite a handicap for a wizard,' Barry said. 'You've done damn well for yourself.'

'Thanks for saying so,' Valumart said. 'How's the book coming?'

'Uh, fine,' Barry lied. He hung up quickly, then told his wife the depressing news.

'There's only one person left to talk to,' Ermine said. 'The foreign professor, Mumblemumble.'

'Oh, what does he know about anything?' Barry said crossly. 'He can't even mix up a batch of Dragonade properly.'

'You know, I'm only trying to help,' Ermine said. 'If I were in your shoes, I'd be a little nicer.'

'You would, would you? Well, you seem to be doing a great job so far!' he grumbled. 'You always think you're so clever – maybe I don't need your help! Maybe I can fix it myself!'

Ermine's temper rose, but she held it in check. Obviously Barry was re-entering adolesence.

'All right,' she said patiently. 'We'll knock off for today. Go and have a drink or squeeze a spot or something.'

'Fine,' Barry said sulkily.

'Tomorrow we hit the Library, bright and early,' Ermine said. Barry stalked off in search of more fodder for his wildly oscillating mood.

*

The next day, the clock was striking noon when Barry walked in.

'Where were you?' he said. 'I looked in the office and you weren't there.'

'I've been here in the Library since eight-thirty,' Ermine said coldly. 'I thought we were going to get an early start?'

'Overslept,' Barry said. He waved a scrap of parchment, the casualty lists from their announcement dinner. 'Nigel's class rank just went up' – Barry counted the casualties – 'twenty-three places!' And that wasn't even counting the Extreme Quiddit plan, which Ermine didn't know about. Nigel would be Head Boy yet! Barry was exultant; like many poor students, he desperately wanted his son to be a whizz. Ermine, on the other hand, having been a young worldbeater herself, expected no less from her first-born. The moral of the story: kids can't win.

'Let's just make sure we don't run out of pupils,' Ermine said. 'Another group of Muddle exchange students has gone missing.' The shifting stairways, spring-loaded bear-trap stairs, and deadly fragmentation floorboards that made Hogwash so fun to read about made it a meat-grinder for Muddles. One wrong step, and you'd end up having to choose between gnawing your own leg off and starvation.

Barry got up; his chair made a scrape, causing a Radishgnaw fourth-year to look up crossly. He blew her a raspberry, just to show the girl who was boss.

'Barry, shh!' Ermine whispered. 'This is a library.'

'I'm going to get Lon,' Barry said, kissing Ermine on the head, and copping a quick feel. 'I convinced Hafwid to let me have him for a while. Swapped him some copper tubing for his still.'

'That stuff will make Hafwid go blind,' Ermine said.

'Too late,' Barry said. 'Have you ever seen the Headmistress of Beaubeaux?'

No matter how many times he saw it, Barry was never quite prepared for the catastrophe that was Hafwid's living quarters. It wasn't a hut, not on purpose – but simply a house that had collapsed and been held semi-upright by the massive amounts of junk piled inside. Imagine the worst bachelor pad you ever saw – now imagine that bachelor roughly eight feet tall and thirty-six stone – and NOW imagine that pad without any toilet facilities of any kind. In fact, happening on Hafwid's early-morning pee was how many female Hogwesians saw their first willy.[38]

[38] This explains the Hogwash tradition of Lesbians Until Graduation. Stark terror was replaced by sweet relief when they finally discovered that your average wizard wasn't quite so, er, expansive.

Barry went to the door and knocked. After there was no answer, he tried to look in the window, but the bright sunlight outside made it impossible to see. He opened the door and stuck his head in. A stench that had, over time, reached the consistency of cheese whacked him across the nose. Barry's burning nostrils unhappily picked out the distinct notes of turned food, stale beer and unwashed giant flesh. There was Hafwid, clothes still on, passed out amid a pile of empties. Neon beer signs provided a ghostly glow; tattered posters of naked giantesses fluttered. The screen of Hafwid's TV (this, along with belching the alphabet, was his main gambit with the ladies – television wasn't allowed at Hogwash) shone blue and moronic. Barry saw Lon asleep in Fing's old bed, curled up and twitching. Occasionally he let out a half-swallowed bark.

'Hey, Lon!' Barry whispered urgently. The dog-man stirred a bit. 'Lon!' Barry repeated, with a little whistle. Suddenly Lon sprang to life, leaping to all fours and letting out a short howl of warning, which was followed by three seconds of frenzied barking to alert his new master to an intruder. Hafwid didn't move a muscle.

'Lon, shut up, it's me,' Barry said. 'Go and check if Hafwid's dead.'

Lon stood up and cleared a path through the empties

as he walked across the room. He licked Hafwid's nose, and felt his breath on his tongue.

'He's okay,' Lon said.

'Then come with me,' Barry said. 'I need a favour from you.'

'Okay, Barry,' Lon said amiably. He really was a good person, and pet. He walked out, then stopped.

'Wait a second.' Lon went to a little chalkboard that Hafwid had pinned to the back of the front door. Barry read the moronic back-and-forth of quotidian life between the roomies. 'We't t'git mor' beere – H.' 'No fud n dish. I ned fud! – L.' 'Gon' t'track. – H' 'Lade cam by for yu – L.' '*ALWUZ* GIT TH' NAMEZ OF TH' LADYS, DICKWEDE! – H.'

Barry noticed that Hafwid took the time to put apostrophes in. Under this last note, Lon wrote, in his painfully slow scrawl, 'Gon whth Barey.Bak latr. – L'

'Okay, I can go now,' Lon said.

'So how is it living with Hafwid?' Barry said. 'You know, you can always stay with Ermine and me in the guest quarters. Ermine would like that.'

'No, it's fine, Barry. I like it. We are outside a lot,' Lon said. 'He doesn't mind when I chew on things.'

'I bet he doesn't even notice,' Barry said.

'The only time I don't like it is when he and his friends make the noises. It hurts my ears.'

'Hafwid's still doing "the bull moose two-step", eh?' Barry said, laughing. He hadn't used that phrase since he'd left school. 'I thought that paternity suit would've calmed him down a bit.'[39]

'He tries not to,' Lon said. 'He tries to go to the track instead. He says it will cost him less money in the long run. I like it. They let me play in the water.' There was an oval moat in Hogsbleede, Hippocamptown Racetrack. Hippocamp racing was a dangerous sport – jockeys were constantly drowning – and a crooked one, too. Hafwid was devoted to all forms of gambling, though not very successful at any of them. 'I got a sistum,' he'd always say – but the cornerstone of each 'sistum' always seemed to involve losing everything.

'Awright,' he'd say, down to his last bet, but with a mad glint in his eye. 'Now I gottum whur I wannum!' He'd lay down that last Gallon more confidently than anybody else Barry ever met – determined that this time

[39] Hafwid was far from the only Hogwash luminary plagued by nuisance lawsuits. Barry didn't even drive any more, after the third time a Muddle claimed whiplash after he saw who the fender-bender was with. Unfortunately for Hafwid, his procreative impulses got rather indiscriminate – some might say 'frenzied' – in the presence of alcohol. And since alcohol was always present, he sowed illegitimate children like dragon's teeth. Worst of all, when an eight-stone woman gives birth to a four-stone, four-foot-tall new-born, it's pretty obvious who the papa is.

would be different, that his luck would change, determined not to learn anything from the past. And then he would lose. But Hafwid never lost his good humour about it, Barry had to give him that (and his bus fare).

He used to take Barry and sometimes Ferd to the track, though later Ferd couldn't go any more, on account of his F.X. Potts' 12-Step programme. The outings always ended at the same restaurant, Victor Crumb's Pantsless Bulgarian Café. It was a rough-and-tumble place that served tough steaks and even tougher customers; Barry wouldn't have dreamed of going in there without Hafwid, but he liked talking to Victor's brother Bob, who drew cartoons. Barry kept one he did for a long time; it showed Barry disappearing down the arse-crack of a woman with freakishly big haunches. (Barry was convinced that it would be worth something some day, but Ermine threw it away 'by mistake'[40] after they got married.) Yes, there were a lot of fond memories – even though he always had to pay for dinner.

'I thought Hafwid was barred from Hippocamptown for trying to fix races,' Barry said. Unfortunately for Hafwid's sake, hippocamps were not susceptible to the usual forms of fixing – being aquatic animals, they could shut their nostrils up tight if you tried to stick a sponge

[40] Twice.

up there; spraying cayenne pepper on their privates was impossible, because even if they had external sex organs the pepper would wash off; Hafwid even tried to paint a fast one to look like its slower brother, but as (bad) luck would have it, that morning it rained.

'Oh, he just sort of squinches down a little and tells them he's you,' Lon said.

Great, Barry thought. I'm now responsible for Hafwid's gambling debts. He saw a future full of dark, oily wizards in pinstriped robes, carrying violin cases with wands in them.

They opened Hogwash's big oak doors (one of which had a small sticker reading, 'No peddling') and walked into the school.

'Anyway, Lon, listen: I need you to help me with something. I'm trying to write down the true story of my adventures, and since you were there too I want you to add things that you remember.'

'Okay, Barry,' Lon said. 'Can we eat something first?'

Chapter Eleven

'HERE'S WHAT *REALLY* HAPPENED . . .'

After swinging by the kitchens, where the house elves gave Lon a bowl of food, the two old friends headed up to the Library.

For such a feckless student, Barry had surprisingly positive memories of the place. First, there were the many hours spent surreptitiously poring over the voluminous section on reproductive biology. It wasn't that Madame Ponce encouraged this type of material – indeed, if she had her way, none of it would've existed at all – but that the raw diversity of humanoid creatures in the magical world meant that *The Joy of Sex* was merely the tip of the iceberg. There was *The Joy of Mer-Sex, The Joy of Elf-Sex, Loving a Goblin, The Gnome's Secret Garden* – Girlrboy Rockhard's profusely illuminated *Copulating with Creatures* set of bestsellers ran to fourteen volumes all by itself! Good, clean fun; as

Bumblemore always said, 'Masturbation is the opiate of the masses.' A curious youngster could ogle for years, and many Hogwesians did. (That, among other things, resulted in them having a worldwide reputation for being a bit fast.) Barry recalled many free periods during first year, skimming for anecdotes that he liked a lot, if not knowing exactly why . . . If there was a picture, he would think about it for days.

Lon and Barry found a quiet spot, two comfortable chairs with a table between them. Barry conjured a pad and pencil for Lon – in Sacramento, a third-grader was made to stand in the corner for forgetting his school supplies AGAIN – and then a copy of all the Barry Trotter books, causing seven different people around the world to be falsely accused of shoplifting.

'So what do we do now?' Lon said.

'Well, I reminisce, and you write it down,' Barry said.

'You what?' Lon said.

'Remember things,' Barry said. Lon's vocabulary was really surprisingly good, considering what he had to work with.

'Okay,' Barry said, opening *Barry Trotter and the Chamberpot of Secrets*. 'Obviously, the Chamberpot was something Bumblemore had, to avoid using the school bathrooms. He was pee-shy.'

'I remember that!' Lon said. 'It looked like you!'

Barry didn't share Lon's enthusiasm. 'Not always. It changed to whoever was on Alpo's shit-list. Like when you rolled in that dead chimera. What the hell were you thinking?'

'It smelled good, Barry.'

'I'm sure it did.' Barry began flipping through the book. 'Oh, now this beginning part is totally wrong, the part with the cake. What I actually did was trick Uncle Vermin's client and his wife into eating their own child.' Barry chuckled. 'Did I ever tell you about that?'

'No,' Lon said.

'Keep writing,' Barry said. 'The Ministry made me put it all right again, the bastards. But those Muddles wondered why their boy was covered with tooth marks.

'This stuff with Dali the house elf – she got his masochism basically right. He used to slam his winky in a drawer. Little beat-up, black-and-blue scrap of flesh, it was.'

Lon shuddered. 'I can't even write that.'

'Just write "WINKY" in the margin, I'll remember,' Barry said. 'Let's see – the Measlys busting me out of the Dimsleys': they didn't use a car, they used plain old C-4 plastic explosive. Jorge got a little enthusiastic and blew off the whole front of the house.'

'I remember that!' Lon said.

'Do you remember the Ministry saying it was the

IRA, and Seamlus O'Stereotype punching me in the gut for "bollocksing up the peace process"?'

'No.'

'Well, I do. Seamlus was – is – a terrible drunk, as you can tell from his name. Beautiful tenor voice, though.'

Barry continued to flip through the book. His nose suddenly crinkled. 'God, what's that awful smell? Lon, was that you?'

'Sorry, Barry. The kitchen gave me cat food instead of dog food. It always makes me do that.'

'Well, if you feel another one coming on, for God's sake run over and aim yourself out the window.'

'Okay, Barry.' Cat food always had a terrible effect on Lon's digestive system. Barry tried to convince him to eat like a person, but Lon wasn't interested. At least he wasn't killing rabbits any more – Ermine had been reading him *Watershit Down*.

'All right. Knocked-up Alley. I remember telling J.G. about this. Awful place, abortions going on wherever you look. Dreadful – glad she changed it. Sometimes the truth is just a little too . . . truthful.' Barry paused. 'I like that. Are you writing this down?'

'Yes,' said Lon.

'Good,' He kept flipping. 'I meet Girlrboy Rockhard, bisexual porn star. He gave me a copy of his book *From*

Fluffer to Fabulous – didn't read it.' Sometimes you don't want the pictures to move, Barry thought. 'Remember that day at Boorish and Clotts? That was the first time that Dad slugged Ludicrous.'

'I remember, Barry,' Lon said. 'Dad always said he wished he'd had his knife.'

'That bookstore went out of business, it's now a Wartytoad's. Good ol' Girlrboy, I wonder what he's doing now? He was the only man I've ever met who parted his pubic hair.'

'I think he's nice,' Lon said.

'You would, Lon. He always let you sniff his bottom, to win points with your mum.' Pages turned. 'Dork Arts and Crafts class ... Rockhard releases the Cornish Hens – ah, here we go: the first time I heard the basilisp.'

Lon shrunk a bit in his chair. 'Barry, do we have to talk about it? He was scary.'

'Oh, he looked scary, but that was just the eye makeup. He was really a harmless old queen. If he doesn't like you, he can paralyse you – but simply with bitchiness.'

Barry remembered one time when the basilisp criticised his outfit. He literally couldn't leave his room for days without second-guessing his fashion sense; then he realised that anybody wearing sunglasses –

indoors! – with canary-yellow lenses shouldn't be casting stones. 'When students started turning up in distant parts of the castle, singing old show tunes, we naturally thought of Snipe – it was a tradition. But eventually we figured out what was going on, with the help of a Bodyjuice Potion.'

'What?' Lon asked.

'Don't you remember it? You drank one, too – it's a mixture of somebody's bodily fluids. Spit, snot, blood, everything; nasty doesn't begin to describe it. Then you look just like them, at least until you throw it up.' For fifteen awful minutes, Barry and Lon were Frabbe and Oyle. 'That's how we discovered that Draco didn't have the Hair of Silverfish. He was a peroxide blond.'

Lon's glassy-eyed gaze had drifted over Barry's shoulder, to a bird sitting on the windowsill. Barry snapped his fingers a couple of times. 'Stay with me, Lon. I can feel my memory eroding.'

'Woof,' Lon said softly, trying to be good. The bird flew away; Lon's attention returned.

'Yada, yada,' Barry said, flipping and feeling his interest ebbing away, too. Why couldn't Rollins's illustrator have made him more buffed-up? 'Valumart's magic dayplanner, Eggnog the spider – Lon, I'll never understand how you could've been afraid of that.'

'It was a huge spider, Barry! I hate spiders!'

'Yeah, but it was wearing a Santa hat!'

'It was still scary,' Lon said. He barked again, louder this time. The same bird had returned, but this time it was wearing a false nose and glasses, in the hope that Lon wouldn't recognise it.

'Shh!' Madame Ponce hissed.

'What do you keep barking at?' Barry asked. 'Do you need to go out?'

'It was another bird,' Lon said. 'He's gone now.'

'Oh,' Barry said, not really comprehending. 'Blah blah blah.' Reading and writing was a drag. Doing the parody was much more fun, Barry thought. I came up with the *ideas*, and the ghostwriter came up with the – what was the word? – *words*.

Barry shut the book. 'I'll fill in the rest later.' If there was a later, Barry thought. 'End it this way: "And so, with the shattering of the last Judy Garland record, I freed Hogwash from the spell of the basilisp. But my fight with Lord Valumart had just begun."'

The pair got up and stretched, before launching into the next book. Lon got on all fours and stretched that way. Seriously, sometimes all he needed was a tail.

'Okay, book three,' Barry said. 'This one's a biggie – do you need to sharpen your pencil?'

'No,' Lon said.

'I have one of those new ball-point quills if you want it,' Barry said.

'No, I'm fine, Barry.'

'Well, take the pencil out of your head-hole,' Barry said. 'It gives me a headache to look at it.'

'Okay,' Lon said. 'I just keep it there so I don't forget.'

Barry cleared his throat and began to flip. 'I remember this one. I started thinking I was going to die after I thought I saw the Phlegm. That's a death omen, a kind of glob of ectoplasm that you see when you're supposed to die. I found a wad of it under my desk in Mrs Tralala's class.'

'Once she predicted I would bite her,' Lon said. 'And she kept trying to trick me into doing it. I was just about to when Professor Sinatra grabbed me and slugged me.'

'The only thing good about Astronomy class is how he'd mix us martinis on the last day of term,' Barry said.

'And let us spit off the North Tower,' Lon said.

'Tralala would never let us do anything fun. Remember how we used to put hot sauce in her inner eye drops?' Barry laughed. 'I've never seen the point of fortune-telling if you can't avoid stuff like that.'

'I didn't like her either. She made Genny wear

glasses.' Tralala was convinced that Genny Measly's third eye had an astigmatism.

'Do you remember when she predicted that girl's first period, right in front of the entire class? That was wrong,' Barry said. 'I laughed so hard I nearly peed myself.'

'Period?'

'Heat, Lon. When she would go in heat, sort of.'

'Oh,' Lon nodded and giggled.

Barry turned back to the book. 'Okay: here I met Serious for the first time. He was in Aztalan for tax revision. Not evasion, Lon, revision, make sure you mark that down – he enchanted his return to get a refund of sixteen billion Gallons.'

Barry leaned back in his chair. 'They accused him of casting all the forbidden spells,[41] but Serious isn't a bad guy, he just cost a lot of people a lot of money with that Hindenware scheme of his. Like Tupperware, but with hydrogen bubbles in the plastic. *Muy explosivo*. And who needs their leftovers to float around, anyway?'

'Wow,' Lon said, not comprehending.

'Yeah, one of his investors was Valumart, who got

[41] These are, very briefly: Aveda Neutrogena, the death-by-moisturising spell; Cruciverba, the death-by-crossword puzzle spell; and Immuppetise, which puts you completely in another person's power.

him thrown in Aztalan. Then after Serious got away from the Marketors – their power was nothing, he was loads more greedy than they were –' Barry leapt to another thought; he got even more distractable as he got younger. 'This was so funny: I once heard a Marketor ask Serious, "Don't you think that's a little manipulative?"'

'Manip . . .?' Lon struggled with the unfamiliar word.

'Forget it, I'll remember it. Anyway, Serious rode this hippogriff named Birkbeck,' Barry said. 'It was amazing – it was simultaneously an animal and an entire college at the University of London.' Barry flipped more pages. He found the part of the book where they'd played Quiddit in a thunderstorm and he'd crashed into Alyssa Spanner, performing an inadvertent episiotomy with his mop. That was around the time when Lon had his accident – he would skip over this part for now. 'Do you remember your familiar? That little travel Scrabble set you had?'

'Yeah, I ate one of the pieces,' Lon said. 'It hurt on the way out.'

'I can imagine. Anyway, that was one of Valumart's henchmen, guy by the name of Pottagoo. He got his, in the end.' As did poor Alyssa, Barry thought. Last anybody heard, she was a witches' rights activist. Barry used to subscribe to her magazine, *Curses*, out of guilt.

'Do you remember the M-Fer's Map? The one we used to get to Hogsbleede?'

'I remember Zonker's.' Zonker's, named after an American cartoon druggy, was the place where unwise Hogwash students would go to get pipeweed from the local Habbits. Barry did it once, but after purchasing a bag of oregano for five Gallons and spending a night going, 'Am I high? I think I'm high. I'm not high. Ermine, am I high?', he decided that butterbourbon was more his style.

'J.G. got the M-Fer's Map all wrong. Yes, the Map showed everybody who was walking around Hogwash, but it also showed what they were doing. If two people were shagging, there was a little beating red heart next to them, for example. This made it absolutely great for blackmail purposes. You know who got around the most? McGoogle! She had a thing going with Angus Filth's cat – before it got paralysed by the basilisp. He told the cat she had fat ankles . . . What was I saying?' Barry asked.

'I don't know,' Lon said honestly.

'The M-Fer's Map, right,' Barry said. 'I used it to sneak out to Hogsbleede. After missing that first trip, I knew I had to go – everybody came back with magical plastic surgery and counterfeiting kits and all sorts of fun stuff. But the best part about the Map, and this was something J.G. couldn't put in the books for obvious reasons, were the ink stamps that came with it. One had a little mushroom cloud on it, and whenever you pressed that down on a place on the Map, a tiny nuclear explosion happened right there. Same with smoke, oil slicks, I think there was even one that did a rain of frogs, but I gave it to some girl . . . Wow, that got us out of some jams.' Barry fondly remembered racing down the halls in the midst of some mischief, slapping the stamp down again and again, the bodies of his hapless pursuers being thrown about like rag dolls – 'Bomb! Bomb! Oil slick! Smoke! Frog! Bomb!'

Wiping a tear from his eye, Barry flipped some more. 'Ah, Professor Drupin, the old Dark Arts and Crafts teacher. You probably don't remember this, because you were in the infirmary getting your brain replaced, but he was a weretrout.'

'What's a weretrout?' Lon asked.

'A weretrout is like a werewolf, but with a trout. Drupin told me later that he probably got attacked, if you can call it that, while fly-fishing in Scotland. Whenever the moon is full, a weretrout turns from a man into a fish. Very dangerous.'

'Why?'

'You know, for somebody who is supposed to be writing, you certainly ask a lot of questions,' Barry said.

Lon had better be getting this all down, because he was definitely forgetting it. 'Dangerous to himself, obviously. Drupin would have to make sure to get himself into a bath and run the taps, or else he'd change, flop around on the ground for a bit, then die. If anybody was foolish enough to get in the bath with him – well, I don't know what would happen. Perhaps they would be bumped aggressively.'

'Oh,' Lon said. 'How could Drupin keep from changing?'

Thank God, he's listening, Barry thought. 'Drupin had to drink this potion that Snipe made for him, and when I say potion, I mean single-malt Scotch. Staying relatively hammered is the only way to keep ichthyanthropy under control, but after about the age of twenty-five, it really takes a toll. That's why he looked like shit, all the time.

'Still, there's something about it that attracts the ladies,' Barry continued. 'He had to beat them off with a stick – and not just the ones who wanted to fillet and fry him up, either.' He picked up the next book, a truly gargantuan tome – J.G. was pumping out pages at an exponential rate.[42] 'Here's where it really gets dodgy.

[42] . . . and readers of *Barry Trotter and the Shameless Parody* know why: the persuasive techniques of her publisher, Fantastic Books. I wonder if applying electrodes to the tenderest bits of Coleridge

First off, the tournament was called "The Advil/IcyHot/Dramamine Quiddit Invitational", not whatever she called it.' Barry paused. 'Is your hand getting tired?'

'From what?' Lon said.

'Writing,' Barry said, trying to hide the upsurge of exasperation. Lon was, after all, doing him a favour.

'Yeah,' Lon said.

'Well, let's finish for today, then,' Barry said. 'Give me the pad. I'll keep it until tomorrow.'

'Okay, Barry,' Lon said, handing over the pad. Lon stowed the pencil in his head, and ambled off, possibly to bite some running water.

Barry wandered through the Library, interrupting a groping session, an unwilling transfer of pocketmoney and some recreational arson, but no actual studying. Finally in the last row in the farthest part of the Restricted Section, he found Ermine. She was sitting at a table piled high with dusty incanabula. The table was bitching loudly. Ermine was kicking it occasionally to make it shut up.

'Having enchanted stuff around can be a real pain,' she said.

would've helped him remember 'Kublai Khan'? 'C'mere, Mozart! You've got a Requiem to finish, and I've got a car battery with your name on it!'

'You just want a table that you can exploit' the table griped.

'Shut your knothole.' Turning to Barry, she asked, 'How did it go?'

'Fine, I think,' Barry said. Ermine held her hand out, and Barry gave her the notepad.

She flipped through it – her look told the story.

'What?' Barry demanded. He grabbed it back, and looked. There, in Lon's blocky, smudgy printing, was the sentence, 'All work and no play makes Lon a dull boy' written over and over. It was arranged in different ways – in the shape of a hydrant, for example, or a bone – but it was always the same.

'I can't believe it,' Barry said. 'All that work, lost.'

'Looks like you've been hoist by your own retard,' Ermine said with a smirk.

Barry didn't reply, fuming.

'I ran into that weird foreign professor today, in the A section of the stacks,' Ermine said, changing the subject.

'Yeah, right,' Barry said. 'You had something planned, didn't you?' he said playfully. Then, in an announcer's voice: 'This bit of adultery is brought to you by Viagra . . .'

Ermine hit him a little. 'Shut up! I was looking up

"antidote"' she said. 'Here's the interesting part: he had a whole armload of books about Atlanta.'

'Why would he be reading about Atlanta?' Barry said.

'Maybe he's one of those . . .' Ermine searched for the word.

'. . . Civil War re-enactors?'

'No.'

'An extremely ill-informed stalker of Martin Luther King?'

'No – anyway, it doesn't matter. I haven't found a cure for you yet,' Ermine said.

'Nothing?' Barry said, suddenly feeling gypped.

'Not really, but these might help,' she said. 'Read some.'

She slid several books over to Barry. The title of the uppermost one was *Market Magic: A Wizard's Guide to Investing*. He sorted through the stack. '*Buying Past Life Insurance? Managing Your 666(k)*?'

'It's a folk remedy,' Ermine said. 'You've heard of being young at heart? We're trying to do the opposite. If you read what old people read, maybe your fogey gland will kick in. Also, I've copied out some phrases for you to repeat before bed.'

Barry opened the scroll she slid over. '"Things were better when I was a kid,"' Barry read aloud.

'Louder – it works better the louder you say it,' Ermine said.

'"Music today is a load of wank!"' Barry yelled, then even louder: '"You like that actress? She looks like a TROLLOP!"' Students started sticking their heads up, looking at the crazy Headmister. Barry was getting into it. '"This VIDEO GAME is giving me MOTION-SICKNESS! It's GOING to ROT your BRAIN!" "This MOVIE is too LOUD!"' The spirit moved Barry and he bellowed, '"KIDS TODAY ARE NO-GOOD, LAZY, OVER-SEXED LAYABOUTS WHO THINK MONEY GROWS ON TREES AND NEVER APPRECIATE ALL THE THINGS THEIR PARENTS DO FOR THEM!"'

The Library was filled with boos, and Barry was showered with wadded-up A4 and rubbers. Every time a missile came his way, his interrobang throbbed. I should really get that removed, he thought for the millionth time.

Sitting down and shielding his face, he said, 'That felt good, Erm. Like it did something.'

Ermine looked up and put her hand on Barry's. 'Oh, darling, do you really think so? Maybe we're not too late.'

Chapter Twelve

YOU'RE ONLY AS OLD AS YOU ACT

Except for the vomiting at the beginning – and, of course, the eventual dying – getting younger was pretty great. Barry's hair was thickening, for one thing. He thought he could see his wrinkles filling in as he brushed his teeth in the morning, but Ermine convinced him it was just poor lighting.[43] It was indisputable that he was losing his butterbourbon gut, and his sex drive was increasing, too – much to the pleasure of Ermine, who had been lying there tapping her foot for years. He was returning to his sexual peak, a place where she had set up housekeeping at the age of seventeen and had never left.

[43] Shaving by candlelight can be a pain in the neck (har har). That's why Bumblemore, Hafwid, Red-Eye Booty and the rest have such long, luxurious beards. Snipe would grow one, but he simply doesn't generate enough testosterone, and Ponce wouldn't loan him any extra.

In fact, for somebody whose goal seemed to be at one point to cobble together a model UN of sexual conquests, Ermine had been completely faithful to Barry during their entire marriage, give or take an occasional dream involving an incubus or six. Instead, she had been sublimating like mad – by teaching Audrey, by fronting a national crusade to pay reparations to house elves, by covering everything she owned in embroidery and appliqué; by starting a home business selling decorative pom-poms for your wand. She had always been a person of tremendous energy, and now every ounce of it was directed towards saving her husband. In return Barry had to perform once, twice, sometimes three times a day. It was, despite the spectre of Barry's impending wink-out, a bit like their honeymoon.

Ermine spent the next several days digging in the Library. Meanwhile, Barry felt better, which was a bad sign. Nurse Pommefritte examined a sheaf of papers and said, 'I would estimate you've dropped to around age fourteen.'

'How can you tell?' Barry asked.

She handed the sheaf of papers back to him. 'Because someone any older than that would consider "Extreme Quiddit" a really bad idea. I can't sign your petition.'

'Fine!' Barry said. 'I'm Headmister, I don't need your permission! We'll do it anyway!' He stomped out. Barry was so angry that he almost slammed into Ermine.

'Barry!' she said. 'I've been looking for you. I think we might have found a cure!'

'Oh yeah?' Barry said.

'Yes, in the United States – Florida – there's a place called the Fountain of Decrepitude. It's by the same people who run the Fountain of Youth, only this one makes you older.'

Sun, sand, bikinis; it all sounded good to Barry. 'Okay, when do we have to leave?'

'Today!' Ermine said. 'The resort is about to close for six weeks – they're between the summer rush and the winter rush.' She pulled him down the hall. 'Don't worry about packing, we'll only be there for a few hours.'

After calculating the time difference, it was clear that time was of the essence – evaporating was too slow, as was travelling snuff. So Ermine decided to cast something she called 'the ol' switcheroo'. Back in their quarters, she conjured a quick fire in the fireplace. Kneeling down to blow on the violet and teal flames, she said, 'All right, when I tell you to, bend over and squish yourself into the fire. Be sure to get your whole body in there. You don't want to leave any body parts behind.'

Suddenly Barry was less excited about this mode of transportation. 'Are you sure it's safe?' he said.

Ermine paused, indignant. 'How would it look if my husband was burned to death because I screwed up a spell?' she said. 'Trust in my perfectionism, okay? Now, GO!'

Barry ducked down, and felt himself go up in smoke extremely quickly. There was a moment or two of blackness, then he found himself reappearing above a man's pipe.

'Blech!' the man said, taking the pipe out of his mouth and looking at it as if it had bitten him.

'No, that's my godfather,' Barry said, brushing the ashes off himself. Frightened, the man ran.

The heat of the day hit Barry immediately; it was a welcome change from Hogwash's supernatural clamminess. Moments later, he saw his wife reappear right on top of a woman. They went down in a heap, and the woman began to sputter and cough. Ermine helped her up, then limped over to Barry.

'You all right?' Barry asked. 'This is a rather full-contact way to get around, isn't it?'

'I just landed funny,' Ermine said. 'Bad timing – she was in the middle of an inhale.'

Ermine pulled out the brochure. 'Now, let's see if I did this right. We should be quite close to the Fountains.'

There was a shop selling roast corn on the cob called 'The Best Ears of Your Life'. Barry suddenly felt peckish – he was always hungry these days, and never gained an ounce. He'd punched extra holes in his old belt until it did two laps around his waist. 'Ermine, do you mind if I get some food?'

'Let's find the Fountain first, Barry,' she said. Sure enough, a short stroll down the miniature streets of the faux Spanish town, and they were greeted by two huge fountains, each sporting a tremendous queue. They stepped to the end of a zigzagging corridor of ropes. 'You must be at least twelve years of age to use this Fountain,' Barry read. It looked like not many people in the line were much older than that.

Taking in the crowd, Barry turned to Ermine and asked, 'Would you mind if I went back and got that corn?'

'I'd be worried you'd lose your place,' Ermine said.

'No sweat – I'd just cut back in with my food,' Barry said.

'You wish,' said a particularly weedy looking twelve-year-old.

'Oh, yeah, big guy?' Barry said. 'Are you going to stop me?'

'Barry,' Ermine said. 'Be mature about it.'

'Yeah, I will,' the kid said. 'I'll wait until I drink the water and get to be about eighteen, get a growth spurt and put on about seventy-five more pounds, and then I'll kick your ass.'

'All right, all right.' Barry was in no mood to bet on this kid's biology. 'Prat,' he mumbled.

'I heard that, whatever it was,' the kid said. 'Get ready for an ass-kicking in' – he referred to the electronic sign posted ahead – 'forty-seven minutes.'

Ermine tried to play the peacemaker; this was like being back at school. 'So why are you going to the Fountain?' she asked the kid, who was busy picking a pimple.

'I wanna learn to drive,' he said, flicking the scrapings at Barry.

Barry grabbed him by the collar and lifted him up. 'Listen: I can make the next forty-seven, now forty-six, minutes of your life seem like an eternity of pain,' he said.

'I know who you are! You're that guy from those movies, Bilbao Baggage!'

The boy began to struggle and yell. Ermine saw some guards look over.

'Put him down, Barry! Right now!' she said.

Barry did so. 'You're so irritating sometimes, Erm, the way you're always sticking up for the little guy.'

We can't get thrown out,' she whispered urgently. The boy was now kicking Barry in the back of the calf over and over. 'Do me a favour and ignore him.'

'Ow! I'll try,' Barry said, wincing with every impact.

'I – hated – your – movies!' the kid chanted as he kicked.

'*Corsicanbros*,' Barry whispered, with a discreet wave of his wand. Suddenly the kid felt each impact himself.

'Ow! Shit!' The game was much less enjoyable now, and so the kid stopped.

As Erm and Barry moved up in the line, they asked people why they were in it. Some wanted to get their pensions early, but most were kids wanting to drive, buy beer, get married, or engage in other dangerous activities sooner rather than later.

'I never realised R-rated movies were such an attraction,' Ermine said to a girl named Meredith.

'Yeah, right,' she said. 'I'm here so I can vote sooner.' Ermine smiled, recognising a kindred spirit.

Freak, Barry thought.

Finally it was Barry's turn to drink. For sanitary reasons, you weren't allowed to drink from the fountain directly; a little woman in a starched white outfit somewhat like a nurse's scooped out a drink's worth into a plastic cup, which she handed over. After drinking the whole thing, the drinker staggered over to some benches to undergo the change. You got to keep the cup. The brochure called it 'a sturdy tankard proudly emblazoned with the park's logo sure to evoke memories for years to come'. (Barry whipped his into some bushes.)

Barry received his cup and took a gulp. It was viscous.

'What the hell is in this?' he asked.

'Magimucil,' the woman said.

Barry didn't follow.

'*Fibre*. You'll need it as you get older.'

Ermine was suddenly very glad she didn't have to drink any; she hated anything that occupied the no-man's-land between drinking and chewing. Ermine gently took Barry's arm and led him over to the benches. Nearby, several park officials were spooning water from the Fountain of Youth into a wrinkly old man in skateboarder's clothes. The boy who had squabbled with Barry in the queue had OD'd. A security guard saw Ermine looking over.

'Happens every day,' he said. 'Got some friends to go through the line for him – took four doses. Said he wanted to get old real quick to beat somebody up. We got here just in time.'

Ermine made a sympathetic face, then turned to her husband, who was running his finger along the sides of the mug, then popping the contents in his mouth.

'Yuck,' he said. 'Any change?'

'None that I can see,' Ermine said. After fifteen minutes, she went and got him another dose – a simple matter now that the park wasn't letting new people in, and the last line of the day was dwindling. Barry and Ermine sat there for an hour or so, until they closed the park, but nothing happened. In fact, Barry swiped the old man's skateboard and did a few tricks – definitely a bad sign. Dejected, they evaporated and spent the evening floating over the Atlantic Ocean.

Whey they got back to Hogwash, they had an unpleasant duty: Nigel required detention. Apparently he had dropped his familiar on to some girl who was sound asleep in Notions class. Her exuberant – nay profoundly hysterical – response had plunged the class into bedlam, and the already overwhelmed substitute decided to make an example of Nigel – not realising that his parents ran the school.

Nigel came in with a swagger. When she heard what he had done, his mum was appalled.

'Dad suggested it,' Nigel said, with a smirk.

Ermine wheeled on her husband, and fired: 'Is this true?'

Barry hemmed a bit. 'Oh, I suppose I might have encouraged Nigel to see the comedic potential in situations like that – you say you dropped your octopus on her head? And she got hysterical because she'd been attacked by the kraken during her trip across the Lake?'[44]

Nigel nodded. Both father and son were sucking in their cheeks in a last-ditch attempt to stave off laughter.

Ermine saw this and didn't share their amusement. Ermine apparated a birching rod, wiping the smiles off their faces – who was going to get it? She handed it to Barry. 'Since you gave him the idea, bright boy, you punish him,' Ermine said. 'Six – no, eight. One for each of Chesterfield's arms.' The octopus in question couldn't bear to watch; he squirted out some ink and the bag at Nigel's waist went black.

Ermine grabbed her keys and bag. 'I'm leaving. I can't bear to watch this,' she said. 'I'll be back in an hour.' She looked at the men in her life, and estimated that their maturity level was about equal – except that

[44] It was rumoured that the kraken wanted her for a hentai video, but this was never proved.

one was an immensely powerful wizard. For her sanity – and maybe the world's safety – she had to cure her husband's youthanasia.

'Well, that was a close one,' Barry said after Ermine left. 'I thought she was going to sit there and watch me do it.'

'Me, too,' Nigel said. 'You aren't – are you?'

'No,' Barry said, making the rod disappear. 'I think I have a more useful punishment. Could you alphabetise my CD collection? I can't find Valid Tumour Alarm's second album.'

Later that evening, shouting above the woofer-bursting rhythms and car-crash harmonies of VTA's breakthrough, 'Planet Anurysm', Ermine immediately proposed another solution. 'Barry, what would you say to taking a bath in the blood of a hundred extremely old women?'

'I would say, "No". Ermine, you really are the Mozart of the revolting idea.'

'Well, bathing in the blood of a hundred virgins is a time-honoured way for witches and wizards to stay young. It's meant to be very invigorating.'

'Projectile vomiting is undoubtedly an excellent cardio workout,' Barry said.

'This book also says it is a good exfoliant,' Ermine

said. 'Look, it's worth a try – if anybody knows how to grow older gracefully, it's Coco Charnel.'

Barry looked at the book. An indisputably perky old biddie with neck-wattles was on the cover.

'Really, Barry – it's not like you have much of a choice.'

'Okay,' Barry said. He either gave in, or died with 'I told you so' being the last thing he ever heard.

Ermine immediately posted a bunch of Blood Drive signs throughout Hogsbleede, asking specifically for women over eighty-five. There weren't many – showgirl isn't a job with a pension – but with Nurse Pommefritte's help and plenty of sweets and apple juice, they were able to get about a quarter bath full. They were going to use the bath in the Guests' Quarters, but decided that it might clog up after it clotted. They borrowed an old laundry cauldron from the house elves instead.

When it came time to submerge, Barry had chugged nearly an entire bottle of Hafwid's most potent home brew – it was the only way he could possibly face what was ahead.

'C'n I wear a bathin' suit?' he slurred.

'Nope,' Ermine said.

'Th'n c'I jus' stan' innit?' Barry asked.

'No, the book says that you have to actually submerge,' Ermine said.

'Wher'?' Barry grabbed for the book. 'Wher' does it say tha? I wanna read it fer myse'f.'

'Wow, you must be really drunk,' said Ermine, keeping the book out of Barry's grasp with ease. 'I've never heard you talk like Hafwid before. Get in!' she said cheerily.

Barry stripped, then looked down at the cauldron. Taking a deep breath, he stuck his foot in. It felt very odd – slightly slippery, but also beginning to coagulate.

'Don't think,' Ermine said. 'The more you think, the worse it will be.'

'Tha's my philosphee uv life,' Barry said, sitting down. 'Agghhh, this is hor'bl.'

'Slop it around on yourself a little,' Ermine said.

Suddenly, the full impact of what he was doing hit him, and Barry's gorge rose – he could take no more. He leapt out of the cauldron and sprinted into the bathroom.

'Careful –' Ermine said, but it was too late; Barry had tracked blood across the carpet. She'd have to get some Spell 'n' Wash from Filth.

The bathroom's acoustics were such that it sounded to Ermine like an entire choir was suffering from food poisoning. After the final number was finished, she tapped on the door and asked, 'Do you feel any older?'

'No,' Barry said weakly. 'But I think I just lost a wisdom tooth.' Then the choir launched into an encore.

The morning after the blood debacle, Ermine said to Barry, 'I have another idea.'

'I don't know if I can survive another one of your ideas,' Barry said, rubbing his sore stomach. He could hardly keep down toast and water. 'I don't have to eat anything, do I? Because I don't think that's happening.'

'No, nothing like that,' Ermine said. 'I just want you to meet someone.'

This someone turned out to be Count Eddie Fowler, the representative of the local Vampires' Union. Eddie was a barber; vampires needed haircuts, too, but no Muddle wanted to keep those kind of hours, so Eddie had a good business.

He and Barry met for lunch around midnight at Vlad's, a Hogsbleede café catering to the local undead. It was a strange place – a typical sort of coffeehouse, lots of exposed brick, track lighting and blond wood, but filled with the most unwholesome sort of things – vampires, zombies, mummies, you name it. If it should've been dead, it hung out (and left rotting pieces of itself) at Vlad's.

'Can I tell you how excited I am to meet you?' Count Eddie said to Barry. 'My kid's read all the books. Well, except for the parody. He hated that.'

Barry's smile became infinitesimally more fixed.

'Could you sign some?' Eddie thumped a pile of paperbacks on the table. A few feet away, a mummy looked in her compact and readjusted her wrappings. 'Make 'em out to Chris. Like I say, he loves 'em all, but he always hopes that you'll die in the end. So you can become a vampire like us. He'll be so excited to hear I've met you. Is it true you're thinking of joining? Do you want a coffee or something?'

'No thanks,' Barry said, scribbling. He'd seen the barista, a zombie, have some of her rotting arm flake off into a latte. 'It's not that I really want to become a vampire, it's that I have this disease – well, we think it's a disease – or spell, maybe somebody put a spell on me – where I can't stop getting younger and younger.'

'Got it. And you think—'

'My wife thinks, really.'

'—and your wife thinks that if you become a vampire, you'll stop getting younger.' Eddie took a sip of his drink (half-whole blood, the rest B+, no platelets, extra plasma, clots sprinkled on the top) then looked at it sceptically. 'I can't believe I forked out over four Gallons for this stuff,' he said. 'Especially when there's so much of it "on the hoof". By the way, thanks for the exchange students – great idea. Gotta be honest, wizards have always tasted funny to me,' Eddie continued. 'No offence.'

'None taken,' Barry said.

'I mean, whatever you grow up eating, that's what you like.' Eddie cleaned the nail of his pinky with a fang. 'I don't know if you'll stop getting younger, and anybody who told you different would be lying to you for the bounty.' Eddie's voice dropped. 'We get a few smackers for every person we "turn". The downside of "turning" people is that you gotta live with them for all eternity – and most people are pretty annoying, so we're getting less and less "new blood".' Eddie smiled at his feeble wordplay, and Barry did too out of courtesy. 'The Ministry of Undeadity has to bribe us, to keep us turning folks, otherwise we'd die out. You'd be surprised at how many vampires fall on stakes every day, or eat garlic by mistake. Example: only last week I had a friend who went to renew his driving licence. He stands in line, gets it done, then walks out into the broad daylight! His last words – "I didn't think it would take that long."' Eddie laughed. 'Dumb son of a bat. You sure you don't want a bone meal biscotti?' Eddie asked. Barry shook his head.

'Anyway, for you, I'd be doing it strictly for the

honour. I'd donate the money to leukaemia research or something.'

'So it's pretty much how it is in the movies? Sleeping all day, roaming around at night, biting people?' Barry asked.

'Yeah, but it's a lot more than that, too,' Eddie said. 'Don't make the mistake of thinking it's like a job, something you can just leave. It's a lifestyle. It's who you are.'

'I see,' Barry said. 'Will I need new clothes?'

'Oh, sure,' the Count said. 'But that's no big deal. Capes and things are cheap, and you can always pick up second-hand stuff, if you don't mind a stake hole or two. There's not a lot of upfront costs, once you deduct your soul.'

Count Eddie paused. 'By the way, can I ask what cologne you wear? It smells terrific.'

'I don't—oh,' Barry said, remembering. *'Des Femmes Anciennes,'* he said, making something up. Count Eddie didn't seem like the type who knew French. 'I guess what I'm wondering the most is, are you happy?'

'No less than any of the other jokers in here,' Eddie said, waving his arm. This was hardly good news, Barry thought. The coffeeshop echoed with moaning and lamentations. The zombies, however, were a lot perkier than their stereotype – turns out all they needed was a little caffeine. A pair of them were playing chess a few tables away.

'You lost a finger,' one said, picking up the digit and handing it to his opponent.

'Stop trying to distract me,' the other zombie said, smiling as he put the finger in the pocket of a tattered, rotting Hogwash blazer.

'Listen,' Count Eddie said, reaching into his back pocket. 'I want to cruise Lovers' Lane before it gets too late, but I don't want you to feel you have to rush your decision. Read this.' He handed Barry a brochure called 'So You Want to Be a Vampire?' which showed a happy, extremely pale family all chasing what looked to be a group of terrified nuns. Judging by the clothing, it was obvious that the pamphlet hadn't been updated since the seventies. Smart, Barry thought – why bring up AIDS if you don't have to?

'Take your time,' the Count said. 'That's the great thing about being a vampire – if you're reasonably careful, you've got for ever.'

'Thanks,' Barry said. 'I'll read it. And thanks for your time, too,' he said, standing up to shake Count Eddie's hand.

'My number's written on the back,' Eddie said. 'Don't call during the day, obviously, but I'd love to hear from you.'

Nice bloke, Barry thought, after Eddie had turned into a bat and flapped away. He noticed a girl at the table next to him, drinking a latte and crying.

Barry wasn't normally curious, but something about this character – a Goth zombie who clearly not too long ago was a human teenager – made asking impossible to resist. Maybe it was the ants trooping in and out of her head wound. 'What's wrong?' Barry said.

'Oh, *everything*,' she said. 'I used to be a student at Hogwash. Last summer, my boyfriend and I broke up, so I decided to kill myself.'

'It was Headmister Malfeasance's fault, wasn't it? He was such a bad Headmister you had to kill yourself, didn't you?' Barry asked.

'No, it was my boyfriend, like I said,' the girl repeated, puzzled. 'We were always talking about how glorious death was, so I thought if I was dead, I could win him back.'

As Barry tried to untangle the logic, the girl kept talking. 'But after I did, a comet passed over the Earth and made me a zombie. Stupid RADIATION!' she yelled, pounding on the table and making the sugar packets bounce. A mummy's head jerked around so quickly it fell off. 'Now what am I going to do? I'm even less popular, everybody I used to hang out with at school runs away from me. I don't have any more brains to blow out, so I'm going to be here for ever!' she sobbed. 'Do you think Stephen and I will get back together? He always liked girls with pale skin.'

'Um . . . maybe,' Barry said. 'I know someone with a hole in his head, and he's very popular.'

The girl leapt at solace. 'Does he want a girlfriend?' she asked.

'Er, no,' Barry said. 'Not unless you smell like a hamburger.'

'Oh, well,' she said.

'How about that guy over there playing chess?' Barry said, pointing at the fellow in the Hogwash blazer.

'No way,' she said. 'He's past due!' Just as he was about to suggest that someone who was undead perhaps shouldn't be so snobbish, Barry noticed a group of aliens walking through the bar tapping people on the shoulder and leading them away.

'Hey!' Barry yelled. 'What about me? What about me, you shits?'

One alien looked at him and shook his head. Several others pointed and laughed, a neat trick with such tiny flat mouths. They even took the zombie girl. Irritated, Barry evaporated without leaving a tip. In a place like Vlad's, you never knew what that might mean.

✲

Back at the room, Ermine was waiting up. Barry told her about the meeting, and they looked at the brochure together. 'Good health benefits,' Ermine said.

'Yeah, but look at the fine print: not available to mortal dependants.'

'Oh, damn,' she said. That's a bit misleading.'

'Funeral expenses are paid for,' Barry said. 'Members' discount on coffins.'

Ermine quoted: 'We buy in BULK and pass the £££ on to You!'

'Tempting. Hey, the resort sounds good.'

'Yes, but who wants to go at night?' Ermine said. 'I don't know about this, Barry. It seems like a huge commitment.'

'Think about the discounts on movies and bus tickets,' Barry said. 'Over a few centuries, that adds up. I'll do it if you'll do it.'

'What about the kids?'

'Nigel will love having vampires as parents,' Barry said. 'He thinks we're boring.'

'I don't know,' Ermine said. 'I think Nigel's going through a bit of a rough time as it is. I think he'd resent it.'

'I suppose you're right.' Barry sighed. 'We would be much cooler than he is.'

'That's not what I meant,' Ermine said. She would be

damn glad when this episode of 'Barry Trotter: Teenage Husband' was over. 'Still, nothing ventured, nothing gained.'

'Yep,' Barry said. 'It's good to have options.' He turned off the light, and Ermine snuggled up behind him.

'I love spooning,' Barry said.

Ermine raised herself up on one arm so he could see her face. 'I prefer to fork,' she said.

After they were finished – it took a while because he had forgotten how – Barry was staring up at the ceiling wondering what age he was. Ermine drowsed on his shoulder, getting an early start on her morning breath, a speciality *de la maison*. In the silence, somebody farted. As Barry giggled, he realised that the end of his nose felt a bit sore. 'Hey Erm, can you see anything on my nose?' Barry asked.

'It's just a pimple,' she said – then they both froze. The Acne of Fire had returned. Barry was losing time faster and faster every day.

Chapter Thirteen

GOOD NEWS, BAD NEWS

Barry awoke the next morning to yet another worrying symptom. Emptying his bladder, he looked down and saw that most of his pubic hair had fallen out. When he showed Ermine, she screamed.

'I'm still legal, I swear!' Barry said. 'I still *feel* legal!' After she had calmed down, Barry turned to Ermine and said, 'You know, what they say is true – it does look bigger without hair.'

If I only have a little while left, Barry thought, I should spend it with my son. So as soon as he dressed (which took some time – his old robes were too big for him, so he was forced to borrow the clothes of a seventh-year who'd run off with a vavavreela), Barry ambled down to the Great Hall, to sit with Nigel and his mates. Unfortunately, there were no mates, there was only Nigel. He had his nose in a book, a choose-your-own-adventure called *Norman Normal and the Curse of the Annual Prostate Exam*.

'Hi, Nigel, mind if I sit?' Barry said.

'Hi Dad. What's "a prostate exam"?' Nigel said.

'A Muddle torture device,' Barry said.

'Oh,' Nigel said. 'Why do Muddles invent stuff like that?'

'I don't know,' Barry said. 'Don't know any better, I expect. They're savages.'

'Hey,' Nigel said. 'Did you hear the good news? I mean, bad news?'

'Well, which is it?' Barry asked.

'You know that roommate I told you about? The one who wore a cape all the time? The one who wanted to meet Art Valumord?'

'Was he a vampire?' Barry asked.

'No, he went insane and jumped off Grittyfloor Tower. That's the bad news.'

'Okay. What's the good news?' Barry asked.

'Whenever a student commits suicide, all his roommates get perfect marks for the term,' Nigel said.

'All right!' Barry said enthusiastically. 'This means you don't have to study any more, right?'

'Right,' Nigel said.

'Then I think I ought to give you my own special education, don't you?'

'Sure,' Nigel said with a wary smile. His dad was acting so weird these days.

'We'll start after breakfast,' Barry said. 'We'll knock off in plenty of time for you to get ready for the Quiddit match.' He whispered to Nigel, 'Did everybody get those lengths of lead pipe I sent via owl post?'

'Yeah,' Nigel said. 'One of the team got it dropped on his head, but he should be okay in time for the match.'

Barry tousled his son's hair in exuberance. Nigel usually hated this, but he was in such a good mood he did it back.

'Hey, Dad, you've grown some hair,' Nigel said. 'It looks good.'

'Thanks,' Barry said, trying not to let his glumness show. Nigel went back to his book. Saturday breakfast in the Great Hall was a fairly leisurely affair; the students slept late, and all the house elves had the day off. This meant that your choices were either cold cereal, toast, or food conjured the night before. As an expert sorcerer, Barry could whip up any food he wanted from the ether, and did so. (A woman in Amiens saw her omelette disappear and blamed her medication; a man in Omsk saw his orange juice vanish and went back to bed.) Toast and cereal Barry obtained the conventional way. The Great Hall toaster had run off with Professor Flipswitch, so the elves had pressed a poor salamander into service – it worked all right, but the lizard always left tracks across the bread. Barry also liked the magnetic milk, which stuck to the metal bowls and couldn't be spilled.

Nigel jabbed his spoon into a whimpering mass. 'If they can teleport a wizard to the moon—'

'I did that to Dorco one time while he was sleeping.'

'– why can't they make a cereal that won't get soggy?' Nigel complained. 'And who thought sentient cornflakes were a good idea? I'd like to bite *him* instead.'

'I know, Nige, but look!' Barry said, turning the bowl upside down.

'That stuff can't be good for you,' Nigel said. 'It tastes like tin.'

Junior walked by with a tray. 'Hi, Nigel, hi Mr Trotter,' he said. 'Can I sit here?'

'Sure,' Barry said.

'Thanks.'

Barry stirred his cereal; Nigel was right, it was soggy. 'Hey, Junior, how's your dad – er, Lee – doing?'

'Fine,' Junior said. 'He's in Chemise Anonymous and back doing FA Cup matches.' The FA Cup[45] was the professional Quiddit league for those louts kicked out of

[45] The second word is 'Awful', and that's all I'm saying.

all the other leagues. It was, as the name suggests, characterised by shoddy play and constant scandal. Lee's father had been arrested several years ago for exposing himself to a group of Muddle year sevens (it was at a science fair – he was disguised as an exhibit on 'hydraulics'), but because he was famous Jardin got off with community service. Amazingly, after an initial dive, the event seemed to help his career; fans now sent him photos of themselves as dirty science fair projects.

'Good, good,' Barry said. 'Nigel told me your good news. Earwigs?'

'*You* know about earwigs?' Junior said, impressed. 'Best thirty Sickies I ever spent!'

'Listen, you may not've heard, but I used to cause a little trouble back in my day,' Barry said. 'Anyway, I wanted to pass some of my secrets on to Nigel after breakfast. Want to come with us to the theme park?' Barry said, then gave them a conspiratorial look, tongue firmly in cheek. 'Can't let my tricks get around.'

Junior beamed. 'That would be really cool, Mr Trotter!'

'Call me Barry,' Barry said, grinning.

The park, located on an island in the middle of the lake, was coming along. When they had approached J.G. Rollins about it, she called it a 'crass obscenity – simply a shoddy way to squeeze a few more Gallons out of my fans'.

'Yes, we know, isn't it great?' said Ludicrous brightly.

J.G. didn't think so, and this meant that if the project was to go forward at all, the Trustees had to come up with a slick end-run. What they decided to do was bold, but risky: 'Hogwash: The Experience' would *not* be based on J.G.'s beloved, sanitised (and definitely licensed) characters, but the real people they were based on – who, as we know, ran the gamut from slightly flawed to absolutely repugnant.

Hogwash: The Experience had been set to open in June, but thanks to 'labour troubles' (the dwarves building the damn thing got offended and refused to work until the height restrictions on the rides were lifted) it was about six months behind schedule. A big Christmas roll-out was being planned. Everybody privately doubted the allure of a roller-coaster in the middle of the winter, but it profited nobody to tell Malfeasance that. 'Let him learn the hard way,' seemed to be the logic, and Barry was right there with them.

'Look, there's the roller-coaster!' Nigel said, pointing to the mammoth first hump of 'Ermine's Wild Libido'. His mum was pretty mad about it, frankly. 'That's ancient history,' she had said. 'I can't understand why everybody makes such a big deal about a little youthful free-spiritedness.'

Barry gave a loud false cough: 'Tramp!'

Ermine had grabbed a section of orange from Nigel's plate and thrown it at her husband. 'Why couldn't it be "Ermine's Voyage of Personal Discovery"?'

'I'm not eating that after it touched Dad's head,' Nigel had said, and the conversation turned to other subjects. But there it was, his mum's entire sexual career, in substandard timber and pre-rusted steel. (Predictably, Malfeasance was the king of corner-cutting.)

'Look, they've almost finished "Hafwid Gets The Spins",' Junior said. 'I think you're supposed to sit in those beer mugs until you summon breakfast.'

'You do what?' Barry said.

'You know, conjure your cookies, cough into the cauldron, call Merlin collect.' He enthusiastically mimed vomiting. Barry had done enough of that lately to consider himself a master of that humblest of arts; Junior had promise, but only if he worked hard.

The boys wandered off, in search of cool scraps, or bugs to pester. All around, the ill-tempered dwarves dug and soldered, painted and paved. Some attractions Barry didn't need to sample, ever – 'Madame Ponce's Cave of Sexual Ambiguity' sprang to mind – but at heart he couldn't wait to see the finished park in all its garish, troubling, death-dealing glory. Then he remembered he would probably wink out before then.

Should he tell Nigel? He and Ermine couldn't decide. They didn't want to upset him – but didn't he have a right to know? Had he noticed? Wouldn't he notice sooner or later anyway? It was a puzzle.

A tentacle holding a waterproof dry-erase board rose up out of the lake. It was the kraken.

'How's it goin'?' the sea creature had scrawled (the marker was hot pink, his favourite colour).

'Oh, fine,' Barry said. 'Actually, not so good.'

The message board disappeared under the waves, then re-emerged. 'Y?'

'I have a curse or something. Youthanasia. It's making me younger.'

'What's wrong with that?'

'Because if I don't stop it, I'll reach age zero and die.'

'O.' Then it re-emerged. 'Sucks 4 U.'

'Hey!' Barry said. 'Thanks for the sympathy, octopussy.'

'Just jokin',' the kraken wrote. 'Does your fam. no?'

'My wife does,' Barry said. 'But my son doesn't. Think I should tell him?'

The board disappeared, then came back after a bit. 'Definitely.'

The kraken spelled quite well, considering, Barry thought. 'Okay, thanks for the advice. I think I will tell Nigel.'

The sign reappeared. 'Pleasure. Could you throw me the other kid?'

Barry laughed. 'No, he's Nige's mate. But check back with me after the Quiddit match.'

'Peace out,' the sign read. The kraken tried to be hip. 'PS – Chesterfield is my nephew.' It disappeared.

Barry called to Nigel, who was busy chunking rocks at some workmen in a pit. 'Nige, come over here.'

'Yeah! All right!' Nigel danced around. 'I just hit one of them on the head!'

'Good jo—I mean, don't do that,' Barry said. Parental discipline had never been his strong suit, but becoming more immature every day wasn't helping, either. 'Nige, I have something to tell you.'

'Dad, I know all about fairies,' Nigel said. 'I saw it on ValuVision. There was this witch with these great big—'

'No, no, it's not that – it's just . . . hm . . . Chesterfield is the kraken's nephew, and he says hi.'

'Is that it? Can I go and throw more stuff?'

'No, wait,' Barry said. 'I . . . there's something . . .' Barry fell silent, and looked at his son thoughtfully.

'Um, Dad, before we both die of old age, okay?'

Barry gave a rueful laugh. 'If only.'

Nigel took a small plastic magnifying glass out of his pocket and started looking at things. 'Nice pimple you've got, Dad.'

'You're not making this any easier.'

'Ow! Crap!' Nigel said, rubbing his eye. 'I looked at that welder. Do you think I'll go blind?'

'No—'

'But if I *did* go blind, then I could get a cool dog—'

Impatient, Barry spat it out: 'Nige, I've got a spell or something on me that's making me younger.'

'Can you still teach me how to drive?' Nigel said.

'Yes, if we do it soon.'

'Okay. I'd get Mum to do it, but she doesn't know how to drive a manual.' Then Nigel stopped. 'Wait, *soon*? What is that supposed to mean?'

'It means I'm dying. I may not live much longer,' Barry said quietly.

Nigel exploded. 'This sodding magic stuff! This fart-sucking, shit-shitting magic!' Nigel wasn't yet truly fluent in profanity, but what he lacked in skill he made up for in feeling. 'I TOLD you that this was bad! I always said, "Don't do spells! You're a spell addict!" Why can't we be normal, like Gran and Gramps?'

'They're not my gran and gramps, Nigel,' Barry said. 'I have to be a wizard – I'm a hundred per cent magical.'

'You're a hundred per cent idiotic, is what you are,' Nigel said, his face crimson. He ticked items off on his fingers. 'Your parents: dead! Bumblemore: gone! Valu-mart: creepy! "Uncle" Serious: running from Astral Revenue! Face it, Dad – everybody who uses magic gets screwed.'

Barry opened his mouth to defend himself, then closed it again.

'What did you do? Do you even *know*? Or did somebody cast something on you and not say anything, just so we could watch you die?'

'That's about the size of it,' Barry said.

'Perfect! We don't even know who the bastard is. Perfect!' Nigel said. 'I'm going to see Mum! I don't want to talk to you any more.' He tromped off, towards the bridge and the school, but not before saying, 'Thanks for ruining my school year, wee wand!'

Junior came up to Barry. 'What's wrong with Nige?'

'Nothing, Junior.'

'So you're one of those families where the kids can call the parents names, and not get slapped?'

'Not usually,' Barry said. 'This is a bit of an exception.' He figured that Nigel could tell Junior himself, if he wanted to. 'Hey, Junior, did your dad/Lee ever tell you about the time we threw piss balloons at Victor Crumb?'

The words 'piss balloons' galvanised Junior's attention. 'No way!'

The pair started to walk across the bridge to the school. 'Yes, way. It was during the World Cup.' Were Barry as mature as he once was, he might've omitted some things on account of Junior's age. But as it was, he divulged every gory detail. '. . . so he finally caught up to us, and trapped me in a stall of the gents'.'

'Did anybody help?' Junior asked.

'No, they just laughed, the bastards!' Barry said. 'Crumb started whaling on me with his mop! And get this: your dad just stood there giving a running commentary!' Barry laughed. He would miss memories like that, once he was dead.

Junior laughed too. 'Mr Trotter, Nigel always said you were cool.'

'He did?' Barry said, genuinely pleased.

Chapter Fourteen

THE END OF AN EXTREMELY SHORT ERA

Though the Grittyfloor Quiddit team kept the details of its genocidal game plan quiet, enough secrets leaked so that the whole school turned out to see what was going to happen. Dorco's reign had been tough on every student not in Silverfish, and now that a pair of Old Grittyflavians were running the school, some longed-for comeuppance was surely in the offing. But nobody had any idea how crushing it was going to be.

A lifetime's worth of head injuries had given the school's Quiddit instructor, Madame Cootch, the mental acuity of a lawn decoration. This meant that Barry, as co-Headmister, would be refereeing the match.

'I'll try to hold off the Silverfish crowd as long as possible,' Barry told the Grittyfloor team in their locker room. 'Sooner or later, their fans are going to riot, so do what you have to do as quickly as possible.'

Junior was sitting in the Top Box, next to Headmistress Cringer.

'I think it's great that you're carrying on the announcing tradition, Don,' Ermine said. 'Your father must be very proud.'

'Dad said he'd pull me out of school if I didn't do it,' Junior said. 'Frankly, Headmistress, I'm with you. Quiddit could bore the socks off a centipede. I'd rather play Muddle Slaughter on my roommate's Hex-Box.'

Ermine frowned. 'That doesn't sound like a very appropriate game,' she said. The bloodlust in the air before every Quiddit match always made her uncomfortable.

'I know! That's why it's fun!' Junior became serious as the teams faced each other. A starting gun was fired (wounding Broadbottom), and the game began.

'The referee releases the balls . . . Silverfish gets the Waffle,' Junior said. 'They advance on goal, putting on speed—'

The crowd gasped, then there was scattered laughter.

'Oh, no!' Don said. 'It appears the Silverfish front line has been decapitated en masse!'

'Surely that can't be legal?' Ermine asked.

'It is,' Don lied – this was *his* role in the scheme. The Headmistress placated, he resumed announcing. 'Here come the medi-wizards. Don't worry, folks, they'll live

– in a jar!' Junior said. Three-quarters of the crowd laughed.

'I find that in very poor taste,' the Bloody Imbecile snarled.

'If Snipe were here, he'd know who to take points from,' said Ludicrous Malfeasance crossly. He'd just been to see Larval in the Infirmary, and had decided to write him off in favour of another clone.

The game continued, and the Silverfish section settled down a bit. Even short-handed, they scored three goals in quick succession, until the Grittyfloor squad put up an invisible palisade of sharpened spikes in front of their goal. After several Silverfishers impaled themselves, the Bloody Imbecile could stand no more. Calling time-out, he leapt out of the box and floated up to Barry.

'Hey, ref, that was a foul!' he said.

'I didn't see anything,' Barry said.

'Neither could they!' the ghost said, brandishing a rulebook. 'Here it is in the book. "Twelve (b): Any team which deploys any invisible obstacles in front of its goal will be charged penalty shots equal to the numbers of players killed or incapacitated."'

'Let me see that,' Barry said, playing it cool. 'This the latest edition? . . . I'll be damned, you're right.' Behind the Baron, the Grittyfloor Basher was fixing a limpet mine to a Silverfish player's mop. Barry blew his whistle. 'Three penalty shots!' Silverfish made all of them. Then the limpet mine exploded, and a portable black hole in the Silverfish goal not only sucked their goalie into another part of the galaxy, it also sucked in the Waffle.

The Grittyfloor squad went wild – it was the first goal they'd scored all year.

'I think something funny is going on,' Ermine said, smelling a familiar rat. 'Barry!' she yelled.

'What?' Barry said. 'I'm busy – I'll talk to you after the match.'

There was only one Silverfish player left, and that was their Sic'er, T. Granville Pus. Even though he was outnumbered, there was no chance that any Grittyfloor player could outfly this ace – especially not their Sic'er, Nigel. Truth be told, Nigel spent the majority of each match upside-down, hanging on to his mop with his knees and fingernails.

'That's why I've got a plan,' Barry had mumbled to his son before the game. 'Nige, don't catch the Sneetch.'

'No worries,' Nigel laughed. He was developing a sense of humour about his poor flying. 'Why?'

'Don't make me explain it,' Barry said. 'That would open me up to legal prosecution. Just stay away.'

So even though catching the Sneetch was Grittyfloor's only chance of winning the match, Pus was the only player who zoomed after it.

'Pus has found the Sneetch – the Grittyfloors haven't picked it up,' Junior said excitedly. 'It's giving Pus a good run for his money.' The crowd held its breath. Ermine had a bad feeling.

'He's got it! Silverfish–'

Suddenly the pitch was rocked by a tremendous explosion. Pus was blown to bits. But when the dust cleared . . .

'I've got it!' Nigel cried. Chance had blown Pus's disembodied right hand, still clutching the Sneetch, to Nigel. Not stopping to consider the grossness, he had made a blind grab for it, and Pus's appendage landed in Nigel's outstretched hand!

'Grittyfloor wins!' Junior shouted. The crowd went crazy. Angry Silverfish students began wading into the other sections, swinging blindly, to vent their frustration. The Bloody Imbecile had Barely Brainless Bill's empty cranium in a headlock, while the victim whipcracked him repeatedly in the face with his wet cerebellum.

'Yuck,' Nigel said, cruising to the ground. He dropped the hand, and was instantly mobbed by his teammates. Meanwhile, the medi-wizards darted to and fro, collecting the scraps of poor Pus.

A less cordial reception awaited Barry when he touched down.

'I suppose you think that was funny?' Ermine said.

'Yeah!' Barry said.

'Several Silverfish students dead, and several others condemned to live in jars of brine – all for a stupid game?'

'Erm, did you see the look on Nigel's face?' Barry said. 'It's more than a game to him right now.' She softened a bit. 'Plus,' Barry continued, 'come on, it's Silverfish, they totally deserved it.'

This infuriated Ermine. 'That's exactly what's wrong with this school – what's *always* been wrong with it!'

'You're cute when the vein pops out of your forehead,' Barry said.

'Shut up about that! Take this whole *thing* with you and Valumart for example,' Ermine railed. 'It's just the same old "my House is better than your House" stuff writ large. It doesn't matter who gets hurt in the process!'

Barry didn't understand. After all, as of that moment, he was thirty-eight going on thirteen. 'Don't be a killjoy,' Barry said. 'You can be such a prude sometimes.'

This was the wrong thing to say to Ermine. '"Prude"? "Prude"? If there's one thing I am not, and have never been, it's a prude!' Ermine yelled. 'But I might as well be, because if you think you're getting anywhere near me for the next month, think again, Mr Quiddit Hero!'

She stomped off. Barry suddenly realised that everybody had been watching. Oh, no, Barry thought. People will think I'm whipped! Quick – some braggadocio: 'Whatever, wiatch!' Barry yelled, and joined the Grittyflavians, who were dumping Dragonade all over his son.

Ermine wasn't the only one to have problems with Grittyfloor's Extreme Quiddit victory. Two days later, Barry and Ermine received an owl from Ludicrous Malfeasance, who demanded their immediate resignations.

'The students are our primary source of revenue,' the letter said. 'You cannot go around killing them. Even in his most megalomaniacal moments, Dorco killed students singly, taking care to make it look like an accident, or pin it on another student. To do any different goes against the dignity of the school and its finest traditions. Headmister Trotter's direct involvement in the wholesale killing and maiming of the

Silverfish Quiddit team was extremely inappropriate. It also cost several Trustees quite a packet.

'In light of your misconduct, the Trustees and I have asked Professor Opla Mumblemumble to replace you as Interim Headmister, effective immediately.'

In a cold rage, Ermine collected her things and left. She was now sleeping in separate quarters from her husband, who was staying up later and later playing Hex-Box anyway. (He was now addicted to Muddle Slaughter.[46]) Barry tried to sneak in once, but Lon had been sleeping in front of the door.

Far from being overwhelmed by becoming Headmister of the world's most famous wizarding school, Professor Mumblemumble took it in his stride. The way he presided over the High Table, the way he squashed all disagreement during dinner, the way he picked food out of his teeth with the gnawed-sharp earpiece of his half-moon glasses, the way he sopped up his gravy with his long white beard and then sucked on it – it was as if Mumblemumble was channelling the spirit of Alpo Bumblemore.

In fact the first thing Ermine had said to her husband

[46] 'Dad, go HOME!' 'Just one more level, Nige. I'm shooting my way through the UN.')

in forty-eight hours was, 'I think Mumblemumble and Bumblemore are the same person.'

Barry wasn't buying it. 'Not *this* again! I refuse to waste my valuable time listening to your crackpot theory,' he said, dropping down below the High Table to play 'fort' with Lon. All further attempts to present her case were met with explosion sounds and fake walkie-talkie talking.

'Crrsht,' Barry said. 'Ermine is a loser, over.'

Lon laughed. 'Yeah! Crrsht, Ermine—'

'Say you copy, spaz!'

'You copy,' Lon said.

'No!' Barry said. 'Oh, forget it.'

Despite all circumstantial evidence to the contrary, it looked like Barry was right, for Headmister Mumblemumble made a very un-Bumblemore-like announcement. Bumblemore believed magic was a talent, like curling your tongue; it could be nurtured, but it couldn't be increased, or even quantified. You either had 'it', or you didn't. So the last thing Bumblemore would ever support was a school-wide standardised test. But that's just what the new Headmister announced.

Mumblemumble spoke from behind the safety of an invisible barrier. 'The test, which you cannot study for, will take place this Saturday, two days from now. It will occupy you for approximately one hour. We are scheduling the test on a Saturday so that you will not miss any of your normal coursework.'

The students greeted this news with a volley of food, which was directed towards an unwitting Barry – Mumblemumble had slanted his invisible barrier.

'Hey! Watch it!' Barry said as the first few missiles slid in. He then grabbed a basket of rolls and began firing back. Mumblemumble continued to talk.

'It is a great honour that Hogwash is the first wizarding school in the world to be chosen for this test, and it is important that each of you do your very best in it. Due to the cancellation of the Quiddit season, thanks to our recent unpleasantness—'

What, does every Headmister have to give me dirty looks? Barry thought, then whipped another roll.

'– the House that has the best cumulative score will win the House Cup.'

I suppose I was wrong, Ermine thought after the announcement, as she listlessly moved vegetables around her golden plate. Then, ever the student: I wonder if I could take that test, too . . . Just to prove I've still got it . . .

Chapter Fifteen

A VIEW FROM THE LEDGER

The next day Ermine was back in the Library, utterly stumped, and depressed. For the first time that she could remember – maybe for the first time ever – the answer she was looking for wasn't there. Or maybe she just couldn't find it. That was too crushing to think about. Since being booted from the position of Headmistress, she had spent every waking minute trying to research a cure. She was angry with Barry, damned angry, and he wasn't going to die before she had a chance to really make him sorry. Oh yes, Ermine was more determined than ever to help Barry live – she'd find a way to make it unpleasant later.

It wasn't that youthanasia was all that advanced – she'd been doing temporal trickery since she was a teenager. Hell, hadn't she kept Paul McCartney as a sort of pet through her entire sixteenth summer? (For him it was just a strange dream, but for her it was a memorable season. She kept him shrunk to three inches tall, getting him wet to make him normal size – who needed that conversation with Mum and Dad? 'Ermine, why is Paul McCartney in the bath?' She ended up having to come clean anyway – she got caught in a summer shower with Paul in her pocket. Her blouse ripped off and she was arrested for indecent exposure. The ride home with her dad redefined 'nightmare'.)

The point was, Ermine Cringer knew her way around Time, knew all its shortcuts and blind alleys, and yet this spell was a brick wall. It had Lord Valumart written all over it. But he had an alibi . . .

Maybe *nobody* did it, maybe it just happened, Ermine thought, skimming her hundredth, maybe two hundredth, tome. Maybe there isn't a cure. Maybe Barry just packed as much life in as he was allowed. After so many dead-ends and promising roads that led nowhere, the seeds of doubt had not only been planted, they had developed into fully grown Shrubs of Doubt, which in turn formed a maze of shrubs, what are those called, I know those have a name – anyway, you know what I mean. Whatever that's called, she was wandering in it, and maybe I should get a better vocabulary or find another line of work.

'The Library will be closing in five minutes,' the

disembodied voice of Madame Ponce said. 'Students will please take any final requests up to the front desk. Anyone using a reference book is required to return it now for reshelving.'

Ermine read faster, hoping to discover the key in the last few minutes of the day. Students walked by her, laughing and joking. 'Rodderick's Reversal' – that sounded promising . . . damn, it only works on cats, what's the point of that? A Temporal Untangle, perhaps . . .?

'Ahem.' Madame Ponce stood there, her thin arms full of books.

Ermine jumped. 'Oh, Madame Ponce, you startled me. I was concentrating rather hard.'

'And what has you studying' – Ponce looked at the book – '*Merlin's Manual* so intently? I'd be shocked if *you* had ever miscast a spell!' she said. Her clothes were, as usual, strangely cut and very drab. She insisted that they be acid-free.

Ermine was determined not to spill the beans until she knew exactly what was going on with Barry. 'Oh, I was just trying to figure out . . . how to quick-age wine for a dinner party.'

Ponce was genuinely alarmed. 'Heavens, don't use *Merlin's Manual* for that! You're liable to turn it into nitroglycerine!' The book's full title was *Merlin's Manual*

For Fixing Major Magical Mishaps, also called the 'M5F2'. It was commonly considered to be the last resort in the direst of circumstances – its remedies were imprecise, impractical and immensely powerful; *Merlin's Manual* dispensed the kind of medicine that killed the patient.

'I have just the book for you,' Ponce said. 'Have you read Nutella's *Forever Slumber*? It's mostly about poisons, but there's a conversion table in the back. I'll have to show it to you tomorrow, though – we're closing.'

Ermine got up. 'All right,' she said. 'Shall I give this to you?'

Ponce shook her head. 'I won't have time to reshelve any more than what I have here – I'm meeting that dashing foreign professor for dinner.' Since when was a balaclava covered in dried food dashing? Ermine thought. 'Put it on the front counter.'

'All right, Madame Ponce,' Ermine said. 'Thanks for your help.'

The librarian smiled, then turned and went down an aisle.

Ermine collected her things and picked up the book – God, it was heavy, and seemed to be vibrating. She remembered how she and her mates used to sit on books for fun. Maybe the book she needed had been misplaced on the shelves. God knows the students rampaged through here like little Vikings. Every evening Madame Ponce would cast an *Atozed* spell, and everything would fly back to its proper place. But by noon the next day, it was a monument to chaos once again.

She put the book on the counter. Maybe if she looked just one more time . . . She slid open a drawer of the catalogue and riffled through its cards. It giggled.

'Shh!' Ermine said, and riffled some more. This time it let out a laugh.

Ponce heard it. Her head appeared out of the aisle. '*Goodnight*, Ermine,' she said, obviously a little annoyed. 'I have to close.' This had been happening since Ermine was a student.

'Sorry, Madame Ponce, just leaving,' Ermine said. She picked up her things to go – when something behind Ponce's circulation desk caught her eye. It was a ledger, upon which was written 'Faculty Use'. Ermine remembered how relentlessly the notices from Madame Ponce would flow if a book were even a moment overdue. If you blocked the mail slot, they would pour in through the chimney, over the transom, under the door . . . You can't recycle magical mail, and anyway who needs that hassle when you can simply buy the bloody book?

That ledger might suggest some new books to try.

Or, Ermine thought, it might reveal who cast the spell on Barry in the first place . . . She *had* to see what was in there.

Some lights went off at the other end of the room – Madame Ponce would be emerging from her aisle any second. Planting her palms firmly on the marble top, Ermine quickly vaulted over the counter and landed next to the high chair that Ponce used to survey all that was going on in the Library. (The slight elevation made it easier for her to zap students absently playing with themselves as they read.) She heard Ponce whistling as she padded quietly toward the front desk – was that 'Book of Love'? To her horror, Ermine realised that her bag was still on the counter. She grabbed the strap and whipped the bag on to the floor, hoping the librarian didn't see. Then she squashed herself into the space under the desk. If Ponce found her – well, what? She was hardly a candidate for detention, but on the other hand, within the Hogwash Library, Madame Ponce was king or queen or something. They probably taught her all sorts of arcane tortures at Library School, thumb-binding, bookmarks thwacked against the soles of the feet, death from a thousand paper-cuts . . . The whistling grew closer, the fluorescent braziers continued to flick off, one by one.

Down on the floor, the dust of a thousand magical tomes fought to get into Ermine's nose. She sneezed.

The whistling stopped. 'Hello? Is anyone there?' Madame Ponce said in a loud voice. When there was no answer she said, 'I remind you that illegally browsing the Library is a castrating offence.[47]' Ermine didn't move; when her breath began to sound loud, she stopped breathing.

After an eternity, Ponce moved away and turned off the main braziers. Ermine could hear the Library door being opened. Ponce stepped over the threshold into the hall, then said, '*Atozed!*' in a forceful voice, slamming the door.

Ermine suddenly felt as if she were trapped inside 'Muddle Slaughter'; the air was filled with books shooting this way and that, some slapping shut before they were carried to their shelves, others reaching such a speed that they flapped in the breeze. Anyone caught in the crossfire would certainly be knocked down; while a paperback might crack a rib, a hardbound edition could put an eye out or knock you unconscious. And a dictionary might kill you, if it hit you right.

[47] While this punishment may seem excessive, it did address what was thought to be the main motivation for staying in the Library after hours: investigating the rumours of a secret stash of ancient pornography filched from the library at Alexandria before it burned.

Still under the desk, Ermine reached up to the counter and began feeling around. She found something with the right heft, but as she tried to pull it down a flying phonebook clipped her on the funny bone. The good news was she was correct – it was the ledger. The bad news was it fell so that the cover got a big, obvious crease down the middle. Ponce would certainly notice; witches weren't Muddles.

It was too late to worry now – Ermine began examining the book. Professor Flipswitch was endlessly improving himself (admittedly a more straightforward thing for a robot, but then again, who *needed* a 'pelvic tractor beam'?). Professor Sprig had checked out hundreds of books on plants, from the common to the exotic; but since they were all apparently from the 'Highs of the World' series, Ermine doubted her interest was strictly academic. Snipe was into crime novels, for reasons now abundantly clear, and Bumblemore . . .

'Wait,' Ermine said aloud. '*Bumblemore?*'

There it was, in Ponce's anal-retentive handwriting: 'Alpo Bumblemore.' And the last entry was from yesterday!

Ermine's heart pounded – her instincts had been right from the start! Opla Mumblemumble and Alpo

Bumblemore were *brothers*! Snipe involved? As if! Only Barry could think of something that idiotic.

What books had he checked out? There didn't seem to be a pattern. *Surviving Humiliation in the Mass Media,* then *How to Stage a Realistic-Looking Fight,* then *Disappearing for Dummies*. Wait a second . . .

Could it be? Could Opla Mumblemumble and Alpo Bumblemore be *the same person*? It made a sort of fiendish, silly, not-very-intelligent sense, perfect for the plot of this book!

And yet Madame Ponce knew. Why would she keep his secret? Something so unholy and perverted flashed into Ermine's mind, she knew it had to be true, using that sort of 'sixth sense' reserved for determining the veracity of unholy, perverted things. To keep her mid-afternoon pick-me-up chocolate bar safely below her tonsils, Ermine turned the page.

There were more books, requested via interlibrary loan: *Conjuring Cash. Muddle Like Me: One Wizard's Two Decades of Deceit. The Wizard Underground.* All these books suggested a life on the lam. *Disguising Yourself as a Bogus Foreigner. Concocting Marginally Effective Pseudonyms.* Being right never got old, she thought, as the books continued to whizz and flutter above her head.

But what about the next one, *Mass Teleportation*?

What was Bumblemore teleporting? It could be anything – gold bars, Thai prostitutes, uncut Peruvian flake . . . There was nothing that old bugger wouldn't do, or Valumart wouldn't fence. Most recently, Bumblemore had checked out travel guides: *Let's Go: Mu, The Nude Beaches of Lemuria* . . . what was the book that Mumblemumble had been putting back when they met in the Restricted Section? It wasn't about Atlanta – it was about *Atlantis*! And there was a final, puzzling one: *Dipstick: An Unauthorised Biography of the Infamous Niccolo of Pollomusca*. Huh?

That's where the record stopped. Ermine didn't know how this all fit with Barry's youthanasia, but with Bumblemore alive and scheming, she was sure he was involved somehow. She sensed it. But why would he want to kill Barry?

Using yet another special sense (what are we up to now, eighth? Ninth?) Ermine suddenly felt like she should get out of there, and quickly. Whatever Bumblemore was doing, it was big, dangerous stuff. But the books . . . She would simply have to take her bibliographical lumps, covering her head and hoping for the best.

Ermine smoothed the cover of the ledger as best she could, then put it on the counter. She sat behind it, with only her eyes peering over the marble, trying to tell whether the books would stop any time soon. After several minutes, she got impatient.

'Bugger this!' Ermine said, vaulting into the maelstrom of literature. Though a whizzing incanabula gave her a nasty bruise, she managed to get out of the Library in one piece.

Now that Barry was younger, he liked to eat an early dinner with the students, and after that go and play on the Hex-Box until they kicked him out. Then he'd go down to Godawfle's Grotto to drink beer and listen to whatever horrible student rock band was striking poses and flailing away earnestly. At some point in his cups, Barry would corner some unlucky student and hold forth on how studying was worthless. 'I did all right, didn't I?' he would slur, leaning in too close and wilting their collars with his beer breath. Students learned to agree, simply to escape. Not that he didn't genuinely change some minds: the OPSTED percentages of the entire school had been sliding steadily downward since his arrival on campus.

Most nights the ex-Headmister would stumble in around four a.m., after spending several hours arguing with some seventh-years over whether taking any job where you had to wear trousers was 'selling out'. So when Ermine went to Barry's room to tell him what she'd discovered, he was nowhere to be found. Even though what she had found out was burning a hole in her brains, Ermine had to keep it to herself, at least temporarily.

We'll confront Alpo tomorrow, she thought, that's what we'll do, and get him to tell us his plan, then threaten to turn him in unless he doesn't reverse whatever spell he put on Barry. Ermine waited up for Barry until she fell asleep.

When he finally came in, a groggy Barry was delighted to find Ermine snuggled in his bed, but in no condition to do anything about it. The upshot of his blurry profanity suggested something about stealing, and Ermine had been his wife long enough to know when to feign sleep.

All right, then, Ermine thought. I'll tell him at breakfast.

Unfortunately, Madame Ponce was an early riser – it wouldn't do for a student to see her padding out of the Headmister's Office in last night's clothes – so Ermine was still fast asleep when her snooping was discovered. As dawn broke, a troop of evil bluebirds in the pay of the Headmister ever so gently pulled back the covers, lifted her up and spirited her away.

Chapter Sixteen

WIZ – X

It was a good thing indeed that Ermine hadn't been able to understand Barry, because if she had, she would've gone through the roof. What the two Trotter males had done was worthy of expulsion. Not that *they* would've cared – Barry would've welcomed an end to the appeals from the Alumni Fund, and Nigel's mixed emotions have been well documented. But Ermine would've been mortified.

Authority had returned; since Professor Mumble-mumble had taken over, it was almost like the old days. No one had died for a solid week, lessons were being taught, if not necessarily learned, and Hogwash was generally a serene and well-functioning institution. Construction was actually accelerating on the theme park, and it looked as though Hogwash: The Experience would make its Christmas deadline with whole hours to spare.

Another thing that made it like the old days was the constant mayhem supervised by Barry Trotter. Though the dissolution of Grittyfloor's Quiddit team after 'Extreme Quiddit' cast an initial pall on the House's chances of winning the House Cup,[48] there were other ways to gain points, most notably by raising money for charity. (Grittyfloor's charity was the local Potions Pantry, which supplied ingredients for curses to hags too poor to afford them.) And with the perennial brake of Severe Snipe finally removed – he could issue all the demerits he wanted from the belly of Aztalan – Barry was determined to win that Cup for Grittyfloor one final time.

Barry selected a group of boys and girls with suitable *joie de vivre* (they cut class a lot) and began passing on what he knew. Though essentially law-abiding – he hadn't any magic to cause trouble with – Nigel was drafted in, of course, and insisted that Junior be included in the gang as well.

[48] Sometime in the misty past of the school, an ancient athletic supporter of unknown origin had been selected as the totem of House dominance. Whose it was, and why it was chosen, was a source of innumerable hours of speculation, most of it too disgusting to examine here.

Barry instructed them in the art of 'rolling' leprechauns for their gold, and which pawnbrokers were stupid enough to take it. He set a few more up in a nice little racket: charging the local dragons for 'protection'. Soon the students got into the spirit and started their own schemes; Junior turned a bunch of aspirins blue, and Nigel sold them to the patrons of the Ho's Head as 'Wizard's Viagra'. Barry was very proud.

Even Hafwid lent a hand. Using his legendary rapport with animals – his secret was letting them bite him as much as they wanted – they set up a Biting Zoo so local children could come to a small paddock near his hut and have animals take mouthfuls out of them. They also harnessed Hafwid's mania for distilling; the giant was always trying to coax a buzz-endowing beverage out of some new substance. Most recently it was daisies, and before that toothpaste.

Hafwid had given Barry and the gang several gallons of the daisy liquor, which they sold at a roadside stand just outside the Hogsbleede city limits (to avoid paying Lord Valumart's rapacious taxes). It was a point of pride that nobody who purchased a cup of 'yellow peril' made it more than thirty feet without collapsing. As usual, Hafwid drank fifty per cent of the supply, but the profit generated by the remainder was more than enough to buy the House Cup, and so Barry and his wards were exultant as they relaxed in Sir Godawfle's Grotto.

'Bugger!' Barry said, transfixed by a pinball game he was playing with Nigel. It was Muddle-themed, and every so often an electronic voice would burble something like, 'You've Just Squeezed Out Another Whelp!' or 'Get a Job!' or 'Look Out! Don't Die!' Barry was sweating and grunting, trying to keep the ball in play – how did Nigel get so good at this? Just as he was about to lose, Barry took his right hand off the flipper and dragged an index finger over the glass, magically moving the ball into a high-scoring socket called 'Your Father Owns the Firm'.

Nigel exploded with indignation. 'Cheat!' he yelled. 'I saw that, you cheated! You used magic to cheat.'

'No I didn't,' Barry said lamely.

'You did!' Nigel said, not backing down. 'I call forfeit. You owe me a Slumgullion Cider.'

'All right,' Barry said, extracting money from the jeans he now wore constantly. 'I was only trying to teach you the value of magic.'

'Yeah, yeah,' Nigel said, and took the coins to the counter.

Slightly deflated over being caught, Barry sought to reinvigorate himself by talking up the next plan. Around the table sat Junior, Barry, eventually Nigel, and an assortment of light-fingered, loose-moralled bit players. Under it lay Lon.

'Now stealing this test won't be easy,' Barry said. 'Actually it could be, but we're going to make it more difficult for dramatic purposes.'

'What do you mean?' Junior asked.

'I could simply cast a C'mere spell and be done with it,' Barry said. 'This new Headmister is a slippy tit, but we've got an advantage: he doesn't know I'm involved. Whatever magic he's put on it, he probably assumes that it's going to be some student trying to steal it, not *the* Barry Trotter.'

'*The* mega-anorak,' Nigel said. He and his dad were now basically like mates. It was weird, but since Barry was about to snuff it, Nigel took what he could get.

'What do you think the Headmister's put on it?' Junior said.

'An Age Barrier, something like that,' Barry said.

'Like what they put on girlie mags, right?' Junior said.

'Right, except infinitely more powerful,' Barry said. 'Mumblemumble is a Master of the Dork Arts and Crafts – and he probably has quite a few porno mags of his own to protect, so he's no beginner. I think I can knock a hole through any spell, but it may take some time, so' – Barry took a swig of his Rhutastic – 'we need a diversion. A big one. I suggest a panty raid.'

'A pantry raid?' asked a student existing only for the purposes of this cheap joke.

'No, no, panty – like underwear,' Barry explained. 'We go around stealing people's underwear. It's an old Muddle custom.'

'Sounds like something a wizard came up with, if you ask me,' Nigel said. 'Presto! You're not wearing any undies!'

Junior thought for a moment. 'I suppose that would work, as a diversion, but wouldn't we get expelled?'

Barry rolled his eyes. 'Expelled, schexpelled. Listen, if I told you half the things I did when I was here . . .'

'Yeah, Dad, but we're not you,' Nigel said. 'We don't have scars and special destinies and income from branded merchandise. We're all just students.'

'Nigel, you're coming with me to steal the test. And the rest of you, if you get caught, I'll say I put you up to it,' Barry said. 'Later I'll cast a spell to remove it from your permanent records.'

The students thought. 'Okay,' they all said.

'Okay,' Nigel said, more warily. He was his mother's son – he knew something would go wrong.

The plan swiftly took shape: using the M-fer's Map,

routes were plotted, and sections designated. To ensure the right level of maniacal glee, Barry instituted a bounty system – five Sickies for a standard pair of shorts, male or female; three for tighty-whities; three for a bra; five for a thong. 'And seven for anything "novelty",' Barry said. 'I'll be the judge and scorekeeper.'

'Do we give the underwear back?' Don asked.

'Will they want it back, after Lon's been at it?' Nigel said.

'I say, give back all undies after counting – except for Silverfish,' Barry said, fully youthanised. He had regressed into the simple tribalism of the student, and it washed over him like a warm bath of disdain. 'Faculty underpants, those go for double. Triple for Snipe's.'

'I still wouldn't touch 'em,' Junior said.

They would do it at night, under cover of darkness; and after dinner, so that people would be woozy after the highly salted, heavy food that the house elves inevitably served.

'Zero-hour is two a.m.,' Barry said. 'No forgetting! Nobody can be on MPT tonight, either.'

'MPT?' Junior asked.

'Magical People's Time,' Nigel said. 'Chronically late.' It was one of his mother's pet peeves.

'Synchronise your timepieces!' Barry said, and a

collection of sundials, waterclocks, and hourglasses were presented.

'Right – we'll meet back here tomorrow morning before the test, to pay out the bounties and try to crack the questions. Good luck! Happy hunting!'

Late that night, as their friends galloped off to pilfer the school's underthings as loudly as possible, Barry and Nigel shared a very special bit of father and son larceny.

'Ow! You stepped on my foot, you ox!'

'Nothing brings family together like a Cape of Invisibility, eh Nige?' Barry said.

Nigel was about to tell his dad just what he could do with togetherness when they got to the door of the Headmister's office.

Barry pulled out the Sneaky Prickoscope, which stayed silent. The coast was clear.

'Cool!' Nigel said with a pleased whisper. 'I gave you that!'

'Shh!' Barry said. 'Who knows what kind of fiendish spells Mumblemumble will have whipped up to protect the test?'

'I don't see what listening at the door will do,' Nigel said.

The boy was right, it was absolutely useless, but

Barry wasn't about to give him the satisfaction. 'Okay, if you're so smart about magic, you go first,' he said.

Now, you might think that, when you're entering the sanctum sanctorum of a powerful wizard with intent to pilfer, it doesn't seem very paternal to send your extremely unmagical son in first. In Barry's defence, thanks to the spell, he had regressed to Nigel's age. In fact, he wouldn't have remembered that Nigel was his son if he hadn't written a note on his left hand: 'The boy with the glasses and the crusty ears is your son Nigel.'

'Fine, I will,' Nigel said. He approached the door-knob as if it were a sleeping cobra. Nigel made several feints at it, until his father gave him a push in the back and said, 'Come on. Just open the bloody door.'

Nigel touched it, and – nothing happened.

He opened the door, and – nothing happened.

Nigel reached for a lamp. Barry slapped his hand away.

'Could be booby-trapped,' he said.

Peering into the dark office, they saw a faint square of light shining around the Headmister's desk. There, on the blotter, was a single piece of parchment.

'I opened the door, now you go and get the exam,' Nigel said sharply. He was still irritated about the whole 'son-I've-caught-a-spell-and-I'm-dying' conversation.

They pulled off the Cape, and Barry walked in. 'Come in, Nige. It's safe,' Barry guessed. He strode briskly towards the desk, until he saw a smeary golden line drawn around it.

'There's your Age Barrier,' Barry said. 'Must've taken him quite a while to lick all the way around that desk. And all that dust-mouth went for nothing, because old Mumblemumble never counted on the great—' Barry tried to walk through and got a wicked shock. Mumblemumble's voice simultaneously boomed out of the darkness:

'Ha! Trotter, you rotter! Try again!'

Barry tried again, and got shocked again, this time even worse.

'Son of a WITCH!' Barry said. The voice laughed.

'Come on, Barry! The test's right there! Come on, Mr Wizard,' it taunted.

Barry reversed to the door, to get a running start. He bounced straight back, and this time the shock was so bad he blacked out for a second. The voice laughed harder and harder. Barry had heard those laughs before – could it be? But he was *dead* ...

'Dad, can I try?' Nigel said.

'No, Nigel, it's too dangerous,' Barry said, his pride coming to the surface of a pain-fogged brain. 'Ahhhh!'

Barry gave a great ululation and slammed himself into the barrier yet again.

'You never knew when you were licked, Rotter,' the voice said. 'Keep it up. Every moment is being recorded for posterity. I'll be watching and laughing at this for years after you're gone!'

As Barry reeled, drooling, his son approached the line. 'Here goes nothing,' Nigel said – and stepped across.

'Dad! I'm in!' Nigel exclaimed.

'Goooo . . . go ge' ih . . . ge' the tesssss . . .' Barry conked out for a tiny snooze.

Nigel grabbed the piece of parchment. He looked at it.

'Dad, this doesn't sound like a test,' he said, then read aloud: '"Dear Muddle! Congratulations on purchasing Wiz-X, the original and best wizard-removal spell on the market. Wizards can cast it, but they can't outlast it! Wiz-X will rid your area of wizards or your money back – guaranteed!

'"Using it is simple: just place this spell somewhere wizards might be lurking – under beds, in cupboards, in your basement or attic – and wait. To magical folk, this spell is a series of ridiculously easy word jumbles; the test promises to transport all those with more than seventy-five per cent correct to the world-famous holiday spot Atlantis. However, in reality, upon casting it they'll be INSTANTLY INCINERATED! (Pardon us for laughing! Ha! Ha!) By the time they realise something's gone wrong, it'll be much too late! And our new Lo-Ash formula makes the clean-up even easier . . ."'

'Dad! Wake up!' Nigel said, stepping back across the Age Barrier to where his father was crumpled. Nigel shook him.

'Huh? Wha? Wassat?' Barry's mind stumbled to life again. There was a singing in his ears, possibly 'The Chipmunk Song'.

'Wake up, Dad,' Nigel said. 'There's something weird about this spell.'

'Weird?' Barry said. There were noises from the corridor outside – screams, followed by laughter, then Mumblemumble's cross voice.

'We'd better leave,' Barry said, his bruised brains slowly coming back to life.

'But Dad,' Nigel protested. 'Look at the test!'

'First we get out of here,' Barry said, clumsily flipping the Cape over them both. They left the room, closing the door quickly. And just in time, too – Mumblemumble was walking down the corridor with a bullhorn in his hand, yelling, 'Whoever pilfered my knickers had bloody well better put them back *right now*!'

Mumblemumble went into his office and shut the door; Barry was sure that he would discover the missing test and sound the alarm, but he didn't. The Headmister simply walked back out again with an odd smile on his face, then shut the door and locked it.

All the way back to Barry's bedroom, Nigel pleaded with his dad to read the spell.

'I will, son, I promise,' Barry said. 'Right now I've got a splitting headache.'

'Don't you believe me?' Nigel said.

'All I believe right now is the pain in my brain,' Barry said, unlocking the door and stepping inside.

'But you've *got* to read it!' Nigel said. 'The test is a spell! The spell is a trap!'

'The test is a who and the trap is a what?' Barry mumbled.

'A trap! A trap! A spell to kill wizards!' Nigel said. His parents *never* took him seriously.

'I'm sure it is, sure it is,' Barry said, pushing his son (who was now roughly his same weight and height) out of the door. 'Tomorrow,' Barry said. 'First thing.'

'Tomorrow's the test!' Nigel yelled. 'It'll be TOO LATE!'

Barry winced. 'Nigel, please keep your voice down. That barrier shocked the crap out of me. I've got a splitting headache and my eyes won't even focus right,' he said. Barry pushed him into the hall.

'Okay, promise you'll take it to Mum first thing tomorrow,' Nigel said.

'Yeah, sure. I will,' Barry said, closing the door. 'She's here. Wait, she's here?'

'Okay!' Nigel said, then ducked back in. 'By the way, why are you and Mum sleeping in separate rooms these days?'

'Uh, I don't think we are any more . . . very confused . . .' Barry said. 'Listen, I'll tell you when you're older.'

'Older? I'm *already* older than you,' Nigel said, put off.

Barry closed the door, and collapsed into bed next to his wife, not even turning off the light. He slept until late the next morning.

Chapter Seventeen

THE BEARDED BABY

At the behest of their master, the Satanic bluebirds brought Ermine in and laid her, ever so gently, in the gondola of the balloon. Then they swooped and dived around her, cooing with cunning, until she was swaddled tightly in her bedclothes, like a mummy.

When the morning light hit her eyes, Ermine was completely disoriented.

'Good morning, Ms Spy,' the Headmister said, stepping away from his telescope. They were in an observation balloon, tethered to the North Tower, floating high above the school.

'Where . . .?'

'I like to come up here every morning and take a look around,' Mumblemumble said, his ridiculous aeronaut robes (complete with a long silk scarf) flapping in the wind. 'It's important that the Headmister keeps an eye on *everything*. Maybe if you and your husband had paid proper attention to the doings of the school instead of sticking your noses in where they didn't belong, you'd still be Headmistress today.' Mumblemumble laughed. 'Oh, who am I kidding? I would've found some way to get rid of you two!'

Mumblemumble snapped his fingers, and they were back in the Headmister's Office. He snapped them again, and he was back in his normal robes. He snapped them *again*, and there was a slice of lemon in his hand. He squeezed it into a cup of tea on his desk, then took a sip through his grotty, food-crusted balaclava.

'No, you aren't dreaming,' he said, anticipating Ermine's question. 'And I'm afraid you've finished sleeping, too.' He mumbled in Latin and did a few jitterbug-style steps. Then he clapped his hands loudly and a tuba appeared in his arms. The old weirdo sat on a stool in the corner and began playing.

'Practice makes perfect,' he said. 'Won't be long.' Ermine sat through an entire rendition of 'The Flight of the Bumblebee'.

'My unofficial theme song,' Mumblemumble said. 'Today is a big day, and I'm a little excited.'

The office around him had reverted to being exactly as it was when Barry and Ermine were students: dark, messy, musty with the accumulated geriatric funkiness of centuries, ringed with shelves crammed with books and curiosities. A crystal skull held down parchments on his desk. Even Sparky the phoenix smouldered drowsily on his perch, just as he had back in the old days.

Ermine became aware that she couldn't move a muscle. This realisation was followed immediately by her customarily fierce morning need to hydrate the porcelain.

'I need to wee,' she said muzzily.

'What?' the Headmister said.

'I need to wee, Alpo. Let me loose, I'll go, and then I promise to let you tie me up again.'

'Alpo? Who is this Alpo you speak of?' the Headmister asked. 'I know no one by that name. As to the other . . .' He waved his hand, and all pressure on Ermine's bladder was gone.[49] Several members of the Silverfish Quiddit team, recuperating in pieces in the school infirmary, suddenly filled their bedpans.

'*Good!*' A student nurse clapped her hands, smiling.

Back in the office, Ermine said, 'Thank you. Now,

[49] This exceedingly useful spell – a variant of which Barry had used, against the Silverfish Quiddit squad – was created by Amos the Semicontinent for use on long car trips, and was responsible for extending the length of Quiddit matches from hours to days and even weeks.

stop this ridiculous charade – most readers figured this out a hundred pages ago. Even the editor was on to you by page a hundred and twenty. Take off your mask, Bumblemore, I know it's you.'

The Headmister considered for a moment. 'What the hell,' he said, and took off his balaclava. Ermine winced – she had never seen such hat-hair before.

Bumblemore didn't notice; he was too busy scratching his beard so vigorously wisps of smoke were rising from it.

'Wow, that's itchy,' he said. He went to a cabinet and opened it, retrieving some salve. He slopped this on his cheeks and chin, making his appearance even more unwholesome.

'The heat rash, my God, there isn't a name for it,' he said, glistening. 'Glad I'll be able to take this off after today.'

'Today? What's happening today? Why are you so excited?'

'The test, of course,' Bumblemore said. 'We're part of a pilot programme. And are we about to fly!' he snickered at this lame witticism. 'I kill me!'

Ermine decided to go for broke. 'Come clean, Alpo. I know all about it – the fight, the disappearance, the disguise, the whole lot,' Ermine said. 'I read about it in the Library.' Then she added, acting on her hunch,

'Why did you put a spell on Barry? If he dies, it'll be murder in the first degree.'

'And a blessing, too,' Bumblemore said. 'The magical world has gone off its nut since your husband wandered out of the womb.'

'Who put you up to it?' Ermine demanded. 'Valumart? He'll let you rot, you know. Money's all that matters to him.'

'You're not so pure in that regard, Miss Cringer,' Bumblemore said. He closed his eyes and Ermine had the strange experience of hearing her voice come out of another person's body. 'Those new Dragonettes are nice . . . I *need* one, Barry, for *safety's* sake!' Bumblemore spoke in his own voice now, and fixed her with a disapproving glare as he did. 'Those mini-dragons are huge, smelly, and horrible for the environment – they burn large swathes of it wherever they go. And as for safety – I bet the poor wizards and witches flying on regular mops next to you wouldn't feel too safe.' Bumblemore saw that his words had touched a nerve. 'So you, too, like to have a little jingle in your jeans.'

Ermine twitched, but not from anger – there were bluebirds walking on her head. 'So you can reverse the spell? Make Barry his normal age again?'

'Nope,' Bumblemore said.

'What do you mean, "nope"?'

'I mean I can't reverse it, it's not reversible – I know, "Ermine's 'Elps" always says, "never cast what you can't uncast" – but oh well. I needed something to keep you two busybodies occupied, and after hearing your husband's absurd comments one night at dinner, I couldn't resist the irony of a case of youthanasia.

'Anyway, with an omelette as ambitious as mine, some eggs are bound to get broken,' Bumblemore said. He suddenly became giddy. 'Can I tell you my plan? This is the part in the book where the villain explains his plan!'

'Villain? Psh. Pathetic loser, maybe.' Ermine wiggled her hands and feet. 'You might as well. I'm obviously not going anywhere.'

A bluebird flew over to Bumblemore's arm. 'Yes, my minions are efficient.' He paused to stroke its head. 'And deadly.'

Ermine couldn't help but laugh.

'Laugh all you want. Who's the immobilised one, Ms Smart? YOU! And who is going to rule the world's wizards after we all get transported to the new kingdom of Atlantis? NOT you!'

There was a pause. 'Are you waiting for me to ask?' Ermine said.

'Yes.'

'Okay, who?'

'ME!' Bumblemore said. 'I, Alpo Bumblemore, will lead the magical race out of this tawdry, dreary Muddle-ridden world to a new and better one! A place we can live in peace, a place far away from all those pea-brained, unmagical, anti-magical clods!' he yelled. The triumphant laugh that followed immediately disintegrated into coughing.

'Alpo, you're a terrible evil villain,' Ermine said. 'Some people can do it, and you just can't.'

'Stumped you pretty well with that spell,' Bumblemore said, hitting Ermine where it hurt. '*Wizard's Workbench* magazine, July 1973 – 'Carl's Cursin' Corner'. I used that picture Colin took of Barry getting on the train. He was happy to supply it. He hates you, you know.'

'It's mutual,' Ermine said. 'Why are you doing this? You've lived in peace with Muddles all your life.'

Bumblemore's eyes flashed. 'In peace? You have an odd definition of that word. But then again, you did grow up in their world,' Bumblemore said. 'Muddles love to fight, and all us magical folk are dragged along for the ride. Who cares what side of an imaginary line you live on? Or whether the postman wears red or blue?'

'That's not fair,' Ermine said. 'Some Muddle wars can't be helped.'

'They should keep 'em to themselves, then.'

Ermine pressed the conjuring coot further. 'But you yourself killed the Dork wizard Grundlemumble in 1945.'

'Don't believe everything you read on the back of a trading card,' Bumblemore sniffed. 'My dear friend Heinz Grundlemumble is alive, well, and a hundred per cent in favour of my plan – the portion he knows about, anyway.'

Ermine strained against her bonds. Bumblemore smiled at her pointless pluck. 'You're young, and young people can be excused some idealism – as long as nobody gets killed over it. I've lived a lot longer than you, and I've had an interest in this topic for decades. Good wars are as rare as Hogwash virgins.'

Ermine was offended. 'Sex is healthy and natural, and I think that —' she began. Bumblemore waved his hand and the room went silent.

'You've had this whole book to talk. Now it's my turn.' Bumblemore played with the Sneaky Prickoscope that Barry had left behind in his office (it buzzed like mad). 'I know my Atlantis plan might strike you as abrupt, but believe me, I've been working on it for years . . . Funny you should bring up Heinz – he's part of how this whole thing started.

'I was born in 1840. For the first seventy-five years

or so of my life, the Muddle country that I found myself in was at peace. I was a talented youth – not unlike yourself – and I enjoyed the quiet. It was very convenient. Because when a Muddle country goes to war, that country's magical folk all pack up and move to safer climes. A bit of a hassle, but it worked for millennia.'

Bumblemore started to make balloon animals, a nervous habit. 'But then the Muddle wars got too big – moving away really didn't work any more. Obviously a magical person can survive nearly anything a Muddle can dish out, if he or she is prepared, but who wants to live like that? We didn't care about the Austro-Hungarian Empire. What did *that* have to do with the price of hemlock?

'After the Great War started – they always called it that, none of us ever saw what was so great about it – the magical authorities from around the world met at Stonehenge and debated what to do. Several of them wanted to separate from the Muddle world then – in hindsight, we probably should've. But I, like you, was young and idealistic, and swayed the group towards staying. Integrated, if you like, but not involved.'

Bumblemore put down a finished giraffe, and started to twist anew. 'It was decided that magical folk living in the countries at war would give their primary allegiance to other magical folk, not to Muddle governments clearly gone insane. The magical way is to let people live by their own lights, and not follow some bemedalled rascal. That's why Terry Valumart is such a creep.'

The balloon Bumblemore was working on popped. 'Damn,' he said, and started another. 'Most of us younger set insinuated ourselves into the various armies, just for something to do. We considered ourselves impartial observers, and did all sorts of things to avoid harming anyone. I got awfully quick with a Memory Charm. And a Bullet-Bender, and a Playing Possum. If I particularly liked some chap, I'd offer to cast a Playing Possum on him so everybody would think he was dead, and then teleport him to somewhere nice, where he could live until the end of the war. I know Grundlemumble was doing the same thing over there for the Germans – we exchanged armoured owls regularly.

'After a couple of months, it was clear what was going to happen. Nothing would be settled, a lot of people would die – mostly Muddles, but a few wizards too – and the whole world would be worse off than before. But at that time I had a lot more faith in the basic decency and goodness of Muddledom than I do now.

'So did Grundlemumble; he wrote to me and said that he believed if there could just be a break in the action, the idiocy of the whole enterprise would become clear and the Muddles would stop killing each other. Nobody wants to die, right? Grundlemumble and I came up with a plan: first, we'd connive to be stationed in the same place. Then, at some prearranged time, we'd wave the white flag from our respective trenches and step out. Then we'd go out and shake hands, swap cigarettes – maybe even do a friendly little waltz. The other soldiers would see this, stop fighting, start laughing, and peace would break out. And once it was there, we thought it would spread. Logical, right?

'We pulled it off: the Christmas Truce. It wasn't easy, mind you; there was one particular sniper who sent at least ten shots my way. "*Excuse* me! White flag!" I would shout. Grundlemumble got a grenade thrown at him. It's so like a Muddle to set up all these rules, then break them whenever it's convenient. That's the first thing you learn with magic – the same rules apply to *everybody*.

'Anyway, we should've taken the hint. Peace did break out, but then after the New Year it was back to war again. I was flabbergasted. Apparently these Muddles *wanted* to kill each other. Sickened, Grundlemumble and I, along with most wizards and witches of our generation, changed our minds – we wanted to move as far away from these bloodthirsty fools as possible. Unfortunately we were not in the majority – intermarriage is a powerful thing – and had to compromise. We magical folk lived among the Muddles, but in secret.

'This was how I lived the majority of my life. It wasn't the perfect solution, but it worked well enough. It created lots of jobs – the entire Ministry of Magicity. Hidden, wizards thrived. Actually I'd like to think that the Muddles benefited from this, too; after all, magical folk need something to do after breakfast has been conjured and the cauldron is scrubbed, so most of the world's great artists and thinkers have been wizards. You don't think Andy Warhol used magic? Every time he sold another soup can for millions, we thought, Surely the Muddles will realise. But they never have. Everybody from Stephen King to Stephen bleedin' Hawking – all wizards.

'Then your blasted husband came along. After those books – and the movies, and the toys, and the deodorant, and all the rest – our cover was blown, there was no going back. And Valumart, once he got a taste, put the wizarding world right in the Muddles' lap, even though he knew better. Even though he knew what Muddles could be like. I'm afraid that living among

num gagged when she saw it, but she
tined for greatness.'
:stiny to yourself,' Ermine said. 'What
else's destinies?'
e Muddles will find some way to kill us
a nuclear war, or drown us through
or freeze us, or infect us, or God
r horrors they'll cook up,' Bumblemore
this way we're controlling our own

Ermine pleaded, 'why not stay? Why
ucate the Muddles? Improve them by
ich them not to be so stupid and greedy
and . . . muddled.'
e,' Bumblemore said. 'It's too deeply
m. I've been trying that tactic for a
y years, and it simply doesn't work.'
)eared tired. 'You'll just have to trust
at his timepiece. 'Anyway, the spell is
st, and there's nothing either one of us
it. I expect you'll want to make a few
re you go – we depart alphabetically,
near the front, obviously . . .'
calls?'
nts,' Bumblemore said. 'And of course
ake some arrangements for your son.'

Muddles has made some of their worst attributes rub off. Greed, for example. Terry Valumart was always greedy, even back at school, but the Muddles have made him much worse.

'While I was at Hogwash, I could live in a little bubble, pretending that Muddles didn't exist. But as soon as I started living amongst them again, I became convinced that it was only a matter of time before they did something designed to kill each other that would kill all of us, too. I think I could survive an ICBM, if I'm wearing a thick enough mac, but I don't want to find out.'

Bumblemore finished a misshapen animal, a sort of a dog with an elephant's trunk. 'Thank you for being so patient, Ermine. I'm almost finished. After Barry couldn't stop the movie, and the real tidal wave hit, I was looking for a way that we magical folk might separate ourselves, as painful as that might be. Then, miraculously, I received a spell in the post – from a Muddle agency, can you believe it? This spell, which I never knew existed, would transport all the world's witches and wizards to Atlantis. They had used something like it once before – my great-great-great-great-great-great-grandfather stayed behind, and so did yours. That's no doubt where we get our blasted idealism.

'So, I knew what I had to do: lead the magical peoples of the world on a permanent holiday. Take them away from those horrible, drab, grasping, stupid Muddles!'

Bumblemore took another gulp of tea. 'Except for tea – I do appreciate them inventing this.

'The spell needed a lot of oomph, it had to be cast en masse – that's a lot of wizard bodies to move – and on the sly, too; if the Ministry had ever found out what I was planning, they'd have a gryphon. They'd probably kill me; no jobs, you see. Bureaucracy's another thing we've picked up from Muddles.

'I only figured it out several weeks ago – I would turn it into a standardised test, and the entire school would cast it at once. All that youthful magical power focused at once would be plenty, and by the time anyone knew what was happening, it would be too late.

'So there you have it,' Bumblemore said. 'Sorry for the monologue.' He waved his hand. 'You can talk now.' Bumblemore released Ermine, who let out a gasp.

'You cast your spells so *tight*,' she said. 'Now that you've told me your evil plans, I suppose you're going to kill me?'

'No, I am going to let you go,' Bumblemore said. 'If you've been listening, you'll know there's nothing evil

Muddles has made some of their worst attributes rub off. Greed, for example. Terry Valumart was always greedy, even back at school, but the Muddles have made him much worse.

'While I was at Hogwash, I could live in a little bubble, pretending that Muddles didn't exist. But as soon as I started living amongst them again, I became convinced that it was only a matter of time before they did something designed to kill each other that would kill all of us, too. I think I could survive an ICBM, if I'm wearing a thick enough mac, but I don't want to find out.'

Bumblemore finished a misshapen animal, a sort of a dog with an elephant's trunk. 'Thank you for being so patient, Ermine. I'm almost finished. After Barry couldn't stop the movie, and the real tidal wave hit, I was looking for a way that we magical folk might separate ourselves, as painful as that might be. Then, miraculously, I received a spell in the post – from a Muddle agency, can you believe it? This spell, which I never knew existed, would transport all the world's witches and wizards to Atlantis. They had used something like it once before – my great-great-great-great-great-great-grandfather stayed behind, and so did yours. That's no doubt where we get our blasted idealism.

'So, I knew what I had to do: lead the magical peoples of the world on a permanent holiday. Take them away from those horrible, drab, grasping, stupid Muddles!'

Bumblemore took another gulp of tea. 'Except for tea – I do appreciate them inventing this.

'The spell needed a lot of oomph, it had to be cast en masse – that's a lot of wizard bodies to move – and on the sly, too; if the Ministry had ever found out what I was planning, they'd have a gryphon. They'd probably kill me; no jobs, you see. Bureaucracy's another thing we've picked up from Muddles.

'I only figured it out several weeks ago – I would turn it into a standardised test, and the entire school would cast it at once. All that youthful magical power focused at once would be plenty, and by the time anyone knew what was happening, it would be too late.

'So there you have it,' Bumblemore said. 'Sorry for the monologue.' He waved his hand. 'You can talk now.' Bumblemore released Ermine, who let out a gasp.

'You cast your spells so *tight,*' she said. 'Now that you've told me your evil plans, I suppose you're going to kill me?'

'No, I am going to let you go,' Bumblemore said. 'If you've been listening, you'll know there's nothing evil about it. Live and let live, I say – with us living somewhere else.'

'I'd say it's evil!' Ermine said. 'Transporting an entire race of people without their knowledge.'

'So it's a little paternalistic. But it's for their own good,' Bumblemore said. 'Atlantis is great – have you seen the brochure?' He fished it out of his robes and shook it with excitement. 'Cabanas on the beach! Breakfast *and* dinner is included!'

Ermine said, 'Doesn't it strike you as odd that there are no Atlanteans around? Even for a visit?'

'They probably want to forget they ever lived in a crap-hole like this,' Bumblemore said.

'What if we get stuck in some interdimensional bus depot, or worse?' She paused, then dived back in. 'You haven't tested this spell – how could you, you wouldn't be here! You're going to risk our lives on this untested spell you got in the post? Bumblemore, I always knew you were foolish and vain, but—'

'Foolish and vain, you say?' Bumblemore raised himself to his full height. 'I may not be famous, girl, but I'm as great a wizard as you'll ever meet. Have you ever seen the trick I do with some newspaper and a jug of water? Foolish and vain,' he sniffed. 'I was born with this beard' – he pulled it for emphasis – 'a very magical sign, that! My mum gagged when she saw it, but she knew I was destined for greatness.'

'Keep your destiny to yourself,' Ermine said. 'What about everyone else's destinies?'

'If we stay, the Muddles will find some way to kill us – burn us up in a nuclear war, or drown us through global warming, or freeze us, or infect us, or God knows what other horrors they'll cook up,' Bumblemore said. 'At least this way we're controlling our own destiny.'

'Alpo, Alpo,' Ermine pleaded, 'why not stay? Why not stay and educate the Muddles? Improve them by our example. Teach them not to be so stupid and greedy and bloodthirsty and . . . muddled.'

'Sorry, Ermine,' Bumblemore said. 'It's too deeply ingrained in them. I've been trying that tactic for a hundred and fifty years, and it simply doesn't work.' Bumblemore appeared tired. 'You'll just have to trust me.' He looked at his timepiece. 'Anyway, the spell is already being cast, and there's nothing either one of us could do to stop it. I expect you'll want to make a few phone calls before you go – we depart alphabetically, you know. C is near the front, obviously . . .'

'A few phone calls?'

'To your parents,' Bumblemore said. 'And of course you'll want to make some arrangements for your son.'

Ermine let out a cry. 'My son? What do you mean?'

'Nigel is a Muddle,' Bumblemore said. 'He'll have to stay behind.'

'I've got to stop it!' she said, and leapt towards the door.

'Ermine, you're overreacting—'

Ermine pointed her wand at Bumblemore. 'One step and I'll moisturise you, old man.' She ran from the room.

'That reminds me, don't forget to bring suntan potion,' Bumblemore called after her. 'Remember, we can't spell utopia without "you" . . . I kill me,' he said, chuckling to himself, and began to pack.

Chapter Eighteen

TRIPPIN'

Ermine ran from Bumblemore's office to Grittyfloor Tower, looking for Nigel. The halls were empty; all the students were taking the exam. When she got to the Common Room, she found Barry, Nigel and Junior carrying suitcases. When the Trotters were reunited, they all began talking at once.

'Erm! I stole the test last night, and it's a trip—'

'Guys! Bumblemore abducted me and told me about this spell, we have to—'

'Mum! Dad thinks I'm crazy, but I think *he's* crazy, because the test is really a trip and the trip is a trap and we have to stop it!'

Barry, in sunglasses with zinc on his nose, pulled rank on his son. 'This test is actually a spell, and it's going to—'

'Transport us to Atlantis,' Ermine said.

'How did you know?' he asked, mouth open. 'Did you steal the test too, you little minx?' Barry chided.

'I just had a long chat – well, a listen anyway – with Headmister Bumblemore.'

'Don't you mean Mumblemumble?' Nigel asked.

'They're the same person,' Ermine said.

Barry's mouth fell open again. His tongue was drying out. 'How—?'

'No time to explain, dear,' Ermine said. 'I need to get a copy of that test. Do you still have yours?'

'Here,' Barry said, handing it over. 'You know what I thought when I read it? Screw you, aliens! You can keep your crummy planets – Barry Trotter's going to *Atlantis*.' Barry pumped his fist vigorously, indicating complete triumph.

'Really?' Ermine said, not paying attention. She handed the sheet to Nigel. 'Nigel, what do you make of this?' He told his mum what he'd read last night.

'I see,' Ermine said. 'And how come you're the only one who sees that?'

'Because I'm a Muddle,' Nigel said, without embarrassment.

Ermine hugged him tight. 'Yes, that's right, you are. We were wrong to try to turn you into a wizard. I know that now.'

After this big, emotional, subplot-resolving moment, Ermine asked, 'Does it say anything else?'

'Only, "if found, please return to Niccolo di Pollomusca".' He handed it back to his mother.

'Barry, do you remember who Niccolo di Pollomusca was?' Ermine said.

'Wasn't he the man who sold me the counterfeit monkey's paw?'

'No,' Ermine said. 'From our History of Magic class.'

'They don't teach us that any more,' Junior said. 'It was replaced by "Marketing to Muddles".'

'Damn that Malfeasance,' Barry muttered.

'Stick with me, Barry. Does "Niccolo the Unwise" ring a bell?'

'No,' Barry said.

'"Niccolo the Annoying"?'

'Nope,' Barry said.

'"Niccolo the Questionable"? "Niccolo the Unmedicated"? "Niccolo the Self-Hating"?'

'That last one sounds vaguely familiar,' Barry said.

'They're all the same man, fool,' Ermine said. 'This spell is the work of none other than Niccolo di Pollomusca, alias Niccolo of the Really Bad Ideas, alias Nicholas Henratty.'

'Nick Henratty!' Nigel said. 'Dad, that's the man from Special Branch! I'll never be able to drink a Coke again!'

'We have to stop everyone from taking the test,' Ermine said.

'It's already started,' Nigel said.

'Then we have to disrupt it, and hope it's not too late.' She pushed up her sleeves – she was still wearing yesterday's clothes, and felt decidedly unfresh. 'You'll need your wands. And I want some black coffee.'

A quarter of an hour later, they stood in a circle, with the test in the middle, surrounded by candles. (Nigel had pilfered them from dead Byron's belongings.) Barry, Ermine, Junior, and Nigel held hands and chanted the following:

Saint Thomas Aquinas, Saint Peter, Saint Paul,
Every last lama, we need y' all.
Each of you imams, and all of you reverends
Help us shift this shit-mountain, yank every lever end!

We're squeezing the Lemon of Power ecumenical
Beseeching the Buddha with chutzpah rabbinical
Singing everyone's praises, from Gospel to Funk:
End Bumblemore's test! Please make them all flunk!

They chanted for several minutes. Occasionally Barry would put on a funny voice, simply to lighten the mood, and Ermine would stamp on his foot. After the chanting was over, it seemed very quiet in the room. There was a long silence, finally broken by Nigel.

'Nothing happened,' he said dejectedly.

'That's not true,' Barry said. 'One candle went out.'

'Sorry, I spit when I talk,' Junior said.

A first-year named Algy came in through the portrait. 'Hi, everybody. What are you doing?'

'Did you take the test?' Ermine asked tensely. 'Is it still going on?'

'Far as I know,' Algy said. 'I finished early – you should've taken it, it was easy.' Algy walked up the staircase to his room. 'See you at lunch!' he said.

Nigel started to cry. 'Mum, Dad – I don't want you to go!'

Ermine grabbed him and started to cry too. 'You go and live with Gran and Gramps, Nigel. Barry and I will find a way back, we promise.'

'But you're going to get burned up!' Nigel said, with the tears really flowing now.

'Shh, shh,' Ermine said, trying to be stronger than she felt. 'If anybody can outwit this spell, it's your father and me. Or at least me.'

'So what do we do now?' Barry said, slightly offended.

Ermine looked at her watch. It was noon. 'Have lunch,' she said, wiping her nose. 'Nigel, you've got a V.B.S.'[50]

❋

[50] Trotter family slang, meaning Visible Bogey Situation.

When they got to the Great Hall, some students were already trickling in – ones who had finished early.

'Swotty bastards,' Nigel said.

'Now do you see why people despise know-it-alls?' Barry asked his wife. 'They cause apocalypses! Apocalyi! Whatever!'

They sat down, and began to eat. Suddenly, Ermine caught a flash in the corner of her eye.

Junior dropped his fork with a clatter. 'That kid – I was looking right at him, and then he disappeared.' There was a small, faintly smouldering pile of dust where Reg Adams used to be.

'Bye, Reg!' somebody called. 'See you on the beach!'

Junior and the Trotters watched in horror as there was a flash, and then another, faster now, then many at once. More kids disappeared – even a few house elves, too.

'What was that kid's last name?' Ermine asked her son.

'Benson, I think.'

By this time the crowd had noticed that the spell was moving alphabetically, and with every new departure they chanted out a name.

'Boodles!'

'Burton!'

'Bumblemore's gone,' Barry said, clapping his hands with glee.

'Pity you won't be able to enjoy it much longer,' Ermine said.

'Killjoy.'

'Barry, if we get out of this somehow, I have two words for you,' Ermine said.

'Long holiday?'

'Yes, but also: home education,' Ermine said. 'This place drives people insane.'

'Carson!'

'Church!'

'Cooper!'

'Cotytto!'[51]

Won't be long now, Ermine thought. Nigel slipped his hand into hers.

An angry kid – an older boy already wearing swimming trunks – burst in. 'Everybody, there's something wrong with the spell!' he yelled. 'Somebody jinxed it! All of the sudden everybody's quills went crazy and started filling in bubbles by themselves!' He held up a narrow strip of paper.

'Let me see that!' another student said, snatching the paper away. There were gasps as it was passed from hand to hand. Finally it got to Barry's table. Sure

[51] Bit ethnic for Hogwash, don't you think? She always claimed it got changed from 'Smith' when they emigrated.

enough, the bubbles had been filled out to read:

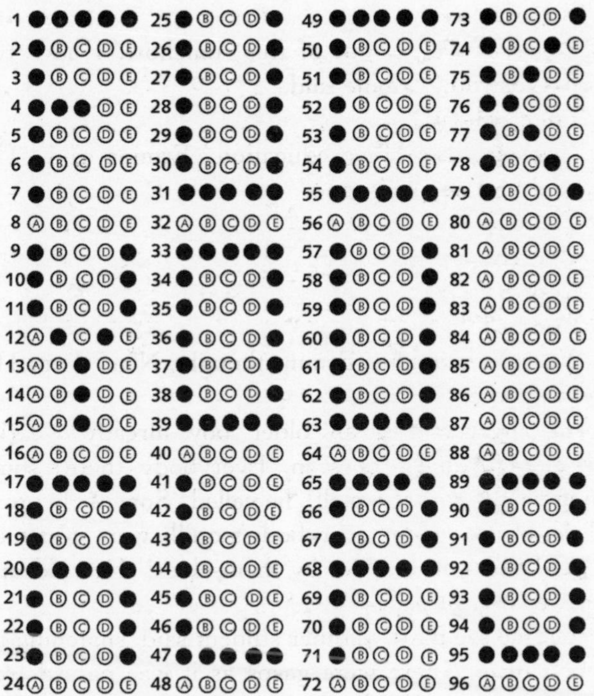

But the disappearances continued – clueless, the house elves were sweeping the ash-piles into a rubbish bag. Then they seemed to slow; had Ermine's *undo* been cast in time?

'Cozzens!'

'Cranagh!'

'Creighton!'

Ermine braced herself. 'Nigel, go and sit by your father!' She squeezed her eyes shut. 'I love you!' she forced out of a tight throat.

. . . and nothing happened.

After a few minutes had passed, and it was clear that the spell had stopped, the students began to boo. Their holiday had been cancelled. The mob knew, instinctively, that Barry Trotter had something to do with it.

'I already blew my allowance on a belching snorkel!' one kid yelled at him. 'Barry Trotter stinks!' another hollered, and it became a chant. Then, oh so predictably, the food started to fly.

'Hey, you,' – a porky girl named Penny Cthulu grabbed Junior – 'I want my knickers back!'

'*Shockadelica,*' Barry murmured, and gave the girl a taser-like tap on the shoulder. She went down, and out. 'We'd better get out of here,' he said. He manoeuvred Ermine, who was still preoccupied with covering Nigel (and occasionally Junior) with kisses, towards the exit. Before closing the door, Barry flipped them the bird. A great wave of rotten food landed – too late.

'You three finish your packing,' Barry said. 'I've got to see a man about a spell.'

Chapter Nineteen

THE BANALITY OF EVIL (OR AT LEAST THIS BOOK)

Barry yanked the Special Branch and leapt down the stairs. Bounding past the receptionist, he neutralised her with a quick Cruciverba Curse; she'd be chasing three-letter words for flightless birds until he removed it. In a trice he was at Henratty's office.

'*Openadoora!*' Barry growled in a high-pitched eleven-year-old voice, wand drawn.

Henratty's door swung open gently. To Barry's amazement, the piles in his office had grown even bigger. Partially concealed by the avalanche pouring out of his in-box, Henratty was on the phone. Looking over the pile, he said, 'Oh, Joan, I'm going to have to call you back. Listen: I leave everything to the kids.' Muffled squawks came from the other end. 'Write it down so you don't forget. No, I can't really wait for you to get a pen. Everything to the kids.' There was some talking from the other end. 'Okay, some to you, too. Whatever you think is best. Also: I have a collection of dirty cloisonné in the shed that I don't want our young Mike to find. Could you destroy them? Yes, sell them on eBuy if you think it'll make some money. I'll explain later. Maybe. Got to go.' More talking from the other end. 'No, really, I mean it. I have to get off the phone. There's a boy standing in my office. He's come to put my arse in a sling, possibly permanently.' More talking. 'Of course he's not more important than you. Listen, which do you think I'd rather do, die, or talk to you? . . . Yes, even about your family. Even talking about your family is better than dying.' Henratty mouthed, 'I'm sorry' and smiled at Barry, who was making the 'wrap it up' gesture with his hand.

'Okay, honey – okay, dear – I'm hanging up now – I'm—Really, I'm—G'bye – Yep. Yep. Sure – G'bye! Bye!' Henratty said, 'Sorry, my wife can really talk. I *used* to think it was cute. Barry, you've lost some weight since I saw you last.'

'And some height,' Barry said, in no mood for banter. 'And some age. Long story.'

'Let me guess, the spell didn't work? Actually, that's obvious – if it had worked, you'd be nestling in a dustbin by now. Oh well.' He walked out from behind the desk, stood in front of Barry and turned around, presenting his bottom.

'What the hell do you think you're doing?' Barry asked. It was hard to sound tough with prepubescent pipes, but Barry did his best.

'I assume you came here to punish me,' Henratty said. 'You win, fair and square. Swish, swish, six of the best, all that.'

'Are you—?' This guy was as crazy as a wizard. 'No! Put your bottom away! I've come here to hear why – solely to satisfy the readers' curiosity, mind you – I don't care. What I'm interested in is killing you.'

'Why? Why should it matter?' Henratty laughed. 'Anyway, you never kill anybody,' he said. 'Do you know how much easier my job would've been if you *had* killed Lord Valumart, just the once? But no, you had to play Gandhi . . .'

Henratty returned to his desk, and continued to talk. 'Of course, when it's a Muddle we're talking about, somebody without a scrap of precious magic in 'em, then suddenly you're Al Capone. I smell a double standard,' Henratty said. 'And let me tell you it doesn't look pretty.'

Suddenly he reached on his desk, grabbed something and threw it at Barry. It was a stress-relieving desk squeezy in the shape of an anvil. It bounced off Barry's chest harmlessly.

'I was going to make a run for it. Oh well . . .'

'Sit down,' Barry ordered. 'And keep your hands where I can see them.' Henratty complied.

'Now tell me, Henratty – what were you planning? And don't try any of your shape-shifter stuff on me.'

'Shape-shifter?' the man asked.

'Come off it!' Barry said, his high voice cracking with volume. 'Hen/rat, it's obvious.'

'Ooookay,' Henratty said, clearly thinking Barry was crackers.

'And that's not even your real name!' Barry said. 'You're really Niccolo di Pollomusca, aka Niccolo the Unwise, aka Niccolo the Improperly Medicated!'

'Wow, you're good,' Henratty said sarcastically. 'Now I know how Valumart feels.' Barry didn't catch the sarcasm.

'All I want to know is, why would you want to destroy the world's wizards? Kill yourself if you want – but taking everybody else with you, that's a dickly thing to do!'

'I'm not a wizard, wisenheimer,' Henratty said, biting a hangnail and examining it briefly before flicking it away. 'I'm just a guy. I got served the Philosopher's Biscotti in 1533 and have been alive ever since.'

Barry was puzzled. 'But why do you hate wizards?'

'If you think the past five hundred years have been fun, you should've paid more attention in History class,' Niccolo said. 'I figured, things have stunk with magical people around, maybe it would be better if they were gone.'

'That's ridiculous!' Barry said.

'Bumblemore felt the same way. That's more than six hundred and thirty years of experience against the opinion of somebody who can no longer vote, drive, screw, or even ride all the rides.'

'That was Bumblemore, he is – was – insane!'

'Maybe so, but you shouldn't blame him for it. I sent him the spell, knowing he couldn't resist.'

Niccolo swung his feet up on the desk. 'It wasn't any grand scheme. My gran found an old trunk in her attic. She hadn't put it there – we figured some local wizard had teleported it there, then forgot it. You people have absolute holes in your heads. Anyway, it was glowing ever so slightly, and seemed to be chuckling to itself, so she sent it to me.

'We opened it and found all sorts of scrolls in it. Most of it was run-of-the-mill stuff – jar-opening spells, incantations to help you do your taxes – but then there was one much older scroll. I sent it to Bumblemore – he's one of our industry contacts – mostly as a joke. It was only after he told me what *he* thought it was that I began to think, Why not let him cast it?'

Niccolo swung his feet down and hunched over his desk, driving his elbows into the cascade of papers. As he talked, he cracked his knuckles. 'Barry, I hate my job. Five people used to do it, but they got downsized. Now there's only me, and you can see how swamped I am. I thought if the spell only works a little – kills one out of every five wizards in England, say – maybe I can catch up. If it works somewhat, I might be able to get ahead. And if it incinerates every magic feeb everywhere ever, then I could retire!'

Henratty smiled and made a friendly gesture. 'See, it's nothing personal.'

Barry was reeling. 'So you were prepared to exterminate an entire race of beings, just because you hate your job?'

'And you condemn a whole race of beings to confusion and misery, just so you don't have to work?' Niccolo paused, to let the irony sink in. 'Why buy something when you can conjure it? Let the Muddles make it, or the house elves! Anyway, let's not get into the morality of magic. I won't convince you, you won't convince me. The point is, as long as there were wizards around, messing things up, I would be stuck here in the office instead of hanging out with my kids or sunning my spare tyre in Ibiza. And the best part is, technically Bumblemore would've done it. I'd just be minding my own business.'

Barry was shocked. 'That's it? No world domination?'

'Nope. That'd be an even bigger hassle. Who needs it? I just wanted to retire,' Niccolo said. 'Do you want an evil cackle or something?'

'It might be nice!' Barry said indignantly. 'This is only the denouement of the entire sodding book. Genocide as a paperwork-reduction method *is* kind of a let-down, yes!'

'It's a good lesson for people to learn. When you get right down to it, life's pretty dull. Anyway, you've never seen our time-share,' Niccolo said. 'The beach is spectacular. You'd have done it, too.'

'Whatever.' Barry raised his wand. 'Any final words?' he asked.

'Yes,' Niccolo said. 'Actually, no. Nearly five hundred years to think of something witty, how embarrassing . . .'

'*Jimhenson!*' Barry said firmly, with a wave of his wand. Niccolo went sort of limp without changing position, and he was making weird swallowed sounds in his throat. Barry raised his left hand and made it into a duck's bill, then opened and closed it.

'. . . the hell have you done to me?'

'It's one of the forbidden spells,' Barry said. 'The seldom-used, not particularly butch, but still very effective "Immuppetis".' Niccolo tried to respond, but without Barry's hand to open and close his mouth, the sounds got stuck in his throat. 'Nifty little spell, really – responsible for my first sexual encounter,' Barry said. 'Now pick up that plastic fork on your desk –' Niccolo had eaten a takeaway curry for lunch. 'And –' Barry mimed stabbing himself in the chest, and Niccolo did so. The plastic fork broke with a weak snap.

'Hmm.' Barry made Niccolo rummage through his desk, looking for something sharp. Niccolo was making those swallowed sounds again. Barry let him speak.

'– to understand. You have no idea how irritating it is to clean up after wizards all day long. Somebody's big-arse BMW touring bike disappears while they're riding it, and who has to go and tell some preposterous lie to the next of kin? Not the wizard, he's off canoodling frauleins on the shoulder of the autobahn! I haven't even had a day off since J. G. Rollins's first book was in galleys!'

Barry made Henratty's mouth close and had him continue to rummage through his desk drawers. Stapler? No. Paper clip? Perhaps if you straightened one out and jammed it above the eye at precisely the right angle . . . Ah, success: a letter opener. That would get to the heart.

He had Niccolo raise it up, paused for drama – and then did something he probably shouldn't have: he let Niccolo speak one final time.

The Muddle was crying now. '– fair! You let Pottagoo go!' he spluttered. 'Go ahead, Mr Famous Wizard, kill the Muddle. Just because he tried to wipe out you and your family.'

'And my friends, don't forget them,' Barry said. 'Technically, you're killing yourself. I'm merely over here minding my own business.'

'Oh, the irony! My own words, thrown back in my face! Seriously, Barry – have mercy. I'm begging you,' Niccolo said. 'I'll never do it again.'

Throughout his life, Barry had always got into trouble when he had thought. Throwing caution to the wind, he did it anyway. He remembered the story Ermine had told him, the one about Bumblemore losing faith in the Muddles, and what she had said to him in return. It sounded like typical Ermine 'let's be nice to people for no reason' crap, but now that he thought about it a bit . . . what did he have to lose? This guy was no Valumart.

'Ah, what the hell,' Barry said, and waved his wand

in an 'X'. '*Delete*,' he said, and Niccolo was released. The man dropped to the floor like a rag doll.

Niccolo staggered to his feet, slipping on a pile of work-orders as he did so.

'Whew,' he said. 'Thanks. I don't know if you've ever cast that on yourself, but it feels like somebody's putting their grubby mitt up your arse.'

Barry turned and walked towards the door. 'Just don't do it again.' He waved his wand. 'By the way,' Barry said, 'I've just made the rest of this week a Bank Holiday.'

'No! You can't –' Niccolo said. 'I mean, the Muddle economy –'

Barry could look surprisingly stern for an eleven-year-old. Niccolo got the point.

'You're right, you're right, I'm calling my travel agent this very minute.'

Outside, in the autumn sunshine, Barry wondered: should I have let him go? Yes, Niccolo deserved to be slit open like a piece of incoming mail, but . . . everybody deserves a second chance, right?

Barry blew the smoke off the end of his wand, holstered it, and hailed the Magic Bus.

Epilogue

A YEAR LATER

Parents' Weekend was ending at St Balthazar's, a beautiful and friendly school known all over Britain as 'the Dentists' Eton'. After a mid-year transfer – something allowed only in the rarest cases – Nigel Trotter had caught up with ease, and was sailing through his second-year with top marks. Professor Maxilla, the school's Headmister, commonly referred to him as 'our prodigy'. Ermine could not have been prouder. And Barry was, too; after all, Nigel had proven himself, and then some. He had saved Hogwash – and probably the rest of the magical world as well. If you do that six weeks into your first year, clearly the school isn't challenging enough. Dentistry interested him, so St Balthazar's it was.

Nigel and his parents had just finished lunch, which was of course accompanied by a vigorous brushing and flossing.

'Did anybody else detect a faint note of fluoride in the crab cake?' Barry asked.

'Oh, they put that in all the food,' Nigel said. 'After a while, you hardly notice.'

The trio reached the Trotters' new Dragonette Decimator, Ermine's reward for thwarting Bumblemore's plan.

She turned to her son. 'Study hard,' she said, kissing him on the cheek. 'We'll see you in a few weeks.' Ermine got into the car, and started it. Barry and Nigel, now taller than his father, walked around to the other side.

'Hey, Dad,' Nigel asked, 'are you ever going to grow up?'

'People have been asking that for years,' Ermine said with a smile.

'From the youthanasia, I mean,' Nigel said.

'Maybe. Who knows?' Barry said. 'I hear they're doing wonderful things with stem cells. Did you know they can grow crotchiness in a petri dish? Anyway, there's no hurry – I stopped getting younger when Bumblemore humped the hellhound.'

Nigel looked puzzled.

'Died, Nige. Get with the hip, happening lingo of the wizards of today!'

'Which you're making up,' Ermine pointed out.

Barry paid no attention. 'Now that I'm used to being underage I like it. People have to do stuff for you.'

Barry got into the car, the passenger's side – he was too young to drive.

'Kiss Fi for me, and tell her thanks for the picture! My mates were totally impressed when it started moving,' Nigel said. He waved goodbye and ran up the hill back to the school.

After they had pulled on to the main road, Ermine asked, 'Do you ever feel sorry for old Bumblemore, now that he's dead?'

Barry laughed. 'Old Headmisters never die, Ermine – you know that,' he said. 'They come back as ghosts in the sequel.'

'When pigs fly!' Ermine said, and that's how they left it.

A THUMBNAIL GUIDE TO THE SORDID SEXUAL ENCOUNTERS EDITED OUT OF THIS BOOK

Now that the book is over, some of you may be wondering, 'Where are the sex scenes? You promised us hot sex scenes, you bastard!' Indeed I did, and had every intention of making *Barry Trotter and the Unnecessary Sequel* a book of sphincter-tightening erotic power. Then I remembered that my grandmothers might read it, and who wants to have *that* conversation?

Because I am a man of my word, I have provided the following guide to the sex scenes that now exist only on my harddrive. Sprinkle them throughout the story, whenever you get bored.

Dramatis Personae	***Comments***
Barry/Ermine	Surprisingly vigorous, considering they're married.
Lon/Valumart's leg	People, fix your pets!
Snipe/greased moccasin	Okay, now that's just *wrong*.
78 House Elves	I hope they washed all the kitchen utensils.
Nigel/*Naughty Nyads* magazine (Oct.)	'I don't think I did it right.'

Earwig/Ahole	Fluttery.
Hafwid/Fistuletta	Let this be a lesson, fellas: don't drink *too* much.
Mumblemore/Ponce	Reading, feeding each other grapes, massive dorkiness.

INDEX

Publisher's Note: In the course of any book, much of the original manuscript falls to the editor's all-conquering blue pencil. This was never more necessary than in the case of *Barry Trotter and the Unnecessary Sequel*. When Mr Gerber's 2,800-page manuscript thumped on our suddenly nauseous doorstep, we naturally assumed that he wanted us to consider it for publication. However, after reading it, we at Gollancz came to believe that the author was following the ancient Roman custom of exposure, where unfit or unwanted offspring are dumped somewhere to die.

When Mr Gerber called to ask about payment (ha!), he called the manuscript 'challenging and postmodern'. We called it 'staggeringly pure crap'. It was only through extensive revisions (done at gunpoint – screw the bloody blue pencil) that this turkey came to be.

Loathe to invest another penny, we are reprinting the index prepared from the original manuscript. As a result, certain incidents and characters mentioned here may not have made it in. We apologize for any confusion, but the sooner we forget the whole experience, the better.